Music for Sight Singing

Fourth Edition

Thomas Benjamin
The Peabody Conservatory
of the Johns Hopkins University

Michael Horvit
Moores School of Music
The University of Houston

Robert Nelson
Moores School of Music
The University of Houston

THOMSON

SCHIRMER

Australia • Canada • Mexico • Singapore • Spain • United Kingdom • United States

THOMSON

SCHIRMER

Music Editor: Clark Baxter
Senior Development Editor: Sharon Adams Poore
Senior Assistant Editor: Julie Yardley
Editorial Assistant: Anne Gittinger
Technology Project Manager: Michelle Vardeman
Marketing Manager: Diane Wenckebach
Marketing Assistant: Rachel Bairstow
Advertising Project Manager: Kelley McAllister
Project Manager, Editorial Production: Emily Smith
Print/Media Buyer: Rebecca Cross

Permissions Editor: Stephanie Lee
Production Service: Stratford Publishing Services
Autographer: Dennis Dieterich Music Publications
   Technologies (for music new to fourth edition)
Compositor: Stratford Publishing Services
Cover Designer: Bill Reuter
Cover Image: PunchStock
Printer: Quebecor World/Dubuque

Printed in the United States of America
1 2 3 4 5 6 7 08 07 06 05 04

For more information about our products, contact us at:
Thomson Learning Academic Resource Center
1-800-423-0563
For permission to use material from this text or product,
submit a request online at
http://www.thomsonrights.com.
Any additional questions about permissions can be
submitted by email to thomsonrights@thomson.com.

Library of Congress Control Number: 2004105363

ISBN 0-534-62802-8

Thomson Schirmer
10 Davis Drive
Belmont, CA 94002-3098
USA

Asia
Thomson Learning
5 Shenton Way #01-01
UIC Building
Singapore 068808

Australia/New Zealand
Thomson Learning
102 Dodds Street
Southbank, Victoria 3006
Australia

Canada
Nelson
1120 Birchmount Road
Toronto, Ontario M1K 5G4
Canada

Europe/Middle East/Africa
Thomson Learning
High Holborn House
50/51 Bedford Row
London WC1R 4LR
United Kingdom

Latin America
Thomson Learning
Seneca, 53
Colonia Polanco
11560 Mexico D.F.
Mexico

Spain/Portugal
Paraninfo
Calle Magallanes, 25
28015 Madrid, Spain

Contents

Part I Common Practice Techniques: Diatonic

Part II Common Practice Techniques: Chromatic

Part III Twentieth-Century Techniques

Preface

Music for Sight Singing is intended to be used over a two- or three-year span. Parts I and II parallel the typical common practice two-year theory sequence. Part III may be integrated into the two-year sequence or may be used in a separate course dealing specifically with twentieth-century materials. The order of *Music for Sight Singing* parallels that of our other texts, *Techniques and Materials of Tonal Music* and *Music for Analysis,* but the text can easily be used with most other theory textbooks. An especially appropriate companion to *Music for Sight Singing* is *Music for Ear Training, CD ROM and Workbook.* Used together, these coordinated materials provide a well rounded, thorough approach to both music reading and aural perception.

As with our earlier texts, *Music for Sight Singing* grew out of our collective teaching experience at the Moores School of Music, The Peabody Conservatory of Music, and the institutions with which we were previously connected. A particular advantage of *Music for Sight Singing* is that the authors are all practicing composers.

The book consists primarily of newly written exercises and melodies that are graded and cumulative and that isolate the particular musical devices under study. Every effort has been made to compose material that is musically and stylistically appropriate as well as pedagogically suitable.

In *Music for Sight Singing,* we have included both part music from the literature and newly composed material. As in our *Music for Analysis,* the music from the literature has been carefully selected to be appropriate and workable at the student's level of progress. We feel that it is important to expose the student to a wide variety of vocal part music from the standard repertoire. All other material has been originally composed to control its content. We have been very careful to compose original material that, in addition to being carefully graded and cumulative, is musical and stylistically diverse.

As the student works through the text, each aspect of music reading is isolated and presented in a specific set of exercises. Problems of rhythm, meter, and pitch are dealt with separately and then together. The melodies and part music are appropriately edited with tempo designations, dynamics, and articulations to encourage the student to deal with all aspects of musical notation while sight singing.

We wish to thank the following people for their help in the preparation of the first edition: Edward Haymes and Luisa Chomel for help with translations; and George S. T. Chu, Hamline University; John C. Nelson, Georgia State University; Dorothy Payne, Department of Music, The University of Texas at Austin; Emily Romney, Longy School of Music, Cambridge, Mass.; and Scott Wilkinson, The University of New Mexico, for their reviews of the manuscript. The reviewers for the second edition were Richard DeVore, Kent State University; Scott Lindroth, Duke University; Rafael Lopez, Community College of Denver; Justus Matthews, CSU Long Beach; and Robert Zierolf, University of Cincinnati. For the third edition, the reviewers were Joel Galand, University of Rochester; Phillip Schroeder, Sam Houston State University; and Robert Zierolf, University of Cincinnati. For this fourth edition, the reviewers were Emelyne M. Bingham, Vanderbilt University; Mark Emile, Utah State University; James Michael Floyd, Baylor University; Richard Hoffman, Belmont University; Geoffrey Kidde, Manhattanville College; Paula Telesco, University of Massachusetts, Lowell; and Barbara K. Wallace, Baylor University.

Thomas Benjamin   Michael Horvit   Robert Nelson

Suggestions to the Teacher and Student

To the Teacher

The following are some suggestions for the optimum use of this book. We have used three types of exercises:

1. *Unpitched rhythmic exercises,* which provide practice with specific rhythmic problems. Included among these are canons and duets. The duets may be performed with individuals or groups on each part. Or each student may perform both parts, either by vocalizing one part and tapping the other, or by tapping both parts, one with each hand.
2. *Pitched preliminary exercises,* which isolate specific melodic and harmonic problems. These should be mastered before going on to the melodies. Preliminary exercises are intended both as a presentation of specific materials and for drill on those materials, as distinct from the melodies and part music. With all material, a balance between sight reading in class and outside preparation is desirable.
3. *Melodies (canons, duets, and trios),* specifically composed to deal in a musical way with material presented in the preliminary exercises.
4. *Sing and Play exercises* are melodies with simple accompaniments drawn from the standard vocal literature. The accompaniments can be played by the singer, other student, or by the teacher. We have presented the melodies without the texts, so that the singer can concentrate on the rhythm and pitches. The use of syllables is strongly recommended. These pieces are readily available in various song anthologies should the teacher wish to perform them with the lyrics. (Students can hone their musical skills by improvising accompaniments to some of the simpler melodies found in each unit.)

Interspersed throughout the exercises are units containing vocal part music from the literature. These provide a more complete musical context for the materials studied thus far.

1. It is important that some material from each section of each unit be covered, and in the proper order. More exercises are contained in each section than most classes will have time to use. It is not necessary to complete all the preliminary exercises before going on to the melodies in each unit. The intent here is to provide teachers with the flexibility to meet their individual needs. Some teachers may wish to make slight reorderings of material (for example, to introduce minor mode a little earlier), but should keep in mind that such reorderings should be done with great care in regard to the selection of exercises. With all material, a balance between sight reading in class and outside preparation (as well as sight-reading practice) is desirable.
2. We strongly recommend that students *conduct* all exercises and melodies after the concept of meter is introduced. The teacher should present preparatory beats, fermatas, and cutoffs. A useful procedure is to have various students conduct the class in the part music. As time permits, and the interest of both class and teacher indicate, it may be useful to go beyond mere "time-beating" to introduce, model, and practice the more contextual aspects of conducting, as this will insure more accurate and musical performances. In this case, issues of the *ictus*; size, speed, and character of the beat; conducting the phrase; approach to cadences; the musical nature of the preparatory beat; and so on should be considered and practiced.

3. In singing pitched material, it is possible to use a variety of methods: fixed or movable *do*, numbers, or a neutral syllable, such as *la*. Tonally oriented systems, such as movable *do* and numbers, work very well in primarily diatonic contexts; however, they lose their efficacy in highly modulatory materials and most twentieth-century idioms.

4. The tessitura of some exercises and melodies may be difficult for some students. These may be sung in any comfortable register or even transposed to a different key at the teacher's discretion. Instrumental as well as vocal idioms have been used to provide students with experience in dealing with the kinds of materials they are likely to encounter in performance situations. In the melodies and part music, emphasis should be placed on both accuracy and musicality of performance, including phrasing, articulation, dynamics, expression, and style.

5. We have employed the normal range of conventional approaches to notation:
   a. Where an incomplete measure occurs at the beginning of an exercise, it is frequently, but not always, balanced metrically in the last measure.
   b. Cautionary accidentals have been indicated both with and without parentheses.
   c. Clef changes within a given melody will occur both within and between phrases.
   d. The variety of notational conventions in twentieth-century music is illustrated in Part III.

6. This book may be used with a wide variety of theory texts currently available. In large measure, it is structured to parallel the organization of the authors' *Techniques and Materials of Tonal Music,* sixth edition (Thomson, 2003), and *Music for Analysis,* fifth edition (Oxford, 2001), and may be used to reinforce the concepts presented therein.

7. Students should be urged to analyze the music they sing in class, including basic melodic shape and structural pitches, harmonic implications, phrase and period structure, cadences, motives, counterpoint, and style.

Because the development of aural skills—the ability to hear and recognize intervals or common chord progressions, to transcribe melodies, and even to hear and transcribe simple pieces—is such an important complementary skill to sight singing, we strongly recommend the use of a companion text, *Music for Ear Training, CD ROM and Workbook* (Schirmer, 2001). The units of text correspond exactly to the units in *Music for Sight Singing,* making the parallel use of both texts especially convenient. And though *Music for Sight Singing* is designed specifically as a sight-singing text, the exercises can be adapted for supplementary use in melodic or rhythmic dictation, using those materials that are not sung in class. The exercises can also be adapted for keyboard harmony by using the melodies for harmonization in a variety of textures and styles.

We recommend that the following suggestions to the student be discussed in class as early as possible in the course.

To the Student

The ability to read accurately and fluently at sight is essential to your musicianship; the competent musician must be able to translate symbol into sound with speed and precision. The exercises in this book have been written and selected to provide you with a wide variety of typical musical problems and to provide exposure to many different styles, materials, and techniques.

You should practice sight reading daily, just as you would practice your own instrument or voice. Steady, disciplined work will yield the best and longest-lasting results. Practice all examples only as fast as you can perform them with accuracy.

Here are some suggestions for practicing and performing the music in this book.

1. *Rhythmic reading.* The rhythmic exercises may be performed in several different ways, for example:

     clapping or tapping the rhythm

     tapping the rhythm while conducting

     vocalizing (as on *ta*) the rhythm while conducting

     tapping the beat with one hand and the rhythm with the other

     tapping or clapping the rhythm while counting aloud the beats in each measure

The rhythmic duets may be performed with one person performing both parts, using a combination of tapping and vocalizing, or with a different person on each part. In general, be as metronomic and rhythmically precise as possible; you may profitably use a metronome while practicing.

Common conducting patterns are shown below. Compound duple meters, such as $\frac{6}{8}$ or $\frac{6}{4}$, are conducted in either 2 or 6, depending on tempo. Compound triple meters may be conducted in either 3 or a subdivided 3, and compound quadruple in either 4 or a subdivided 4. In slow tempos, simple meters may be conducted with a divided beat.

Quintuple meters, such as $\frac{5}{4}$, may be conducted as shown in the illustration, or as combinations of duple and triple meters. Similarly, septuple meters, such as $\frac{7}{4}$, may be conducted as a combination of duple, triple, and/or quadruple. The specific pattern chosen will reflect the prevailing rhythmic distribution within each bar.

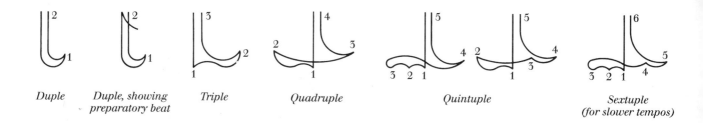

Duple   Duple, showing   Triple   Quadruple   Quintuple   Sextuple
               preparatory beat   (for slower tempos)

Your beat-patterns should be very clear as to the placement of each beat (the arrival, or *ictus*), not too large, of roughly equal size, and uniform in speed within the tempo. Your teacher may choose to work with you on expressive conducting, in which the beat (including the preliminary beat) reflects character, dynamic, phrase-length, expression, and style.

2. *Reading of melodies and part music.* This is one possible technique for sight singing:

     a. Note the meter signature and decide on an appropriate conducting pattern. Look up any unfamiliar tempo designations in the glossary.

     b. Find, analyze, and drill any rhythmic problems.

     c. Determine the key and play the tonic pitch on a piano or other instrument. Sing the tonic triad, and find the first note of the melody.

     d. Sing and conduct through the exercise at a moderate tempo, concentrating on accuracy of pitch and rhythm. Mark breathing places.

     e. Isolate and drill any pitch problems. Use the piano or instrument very sparingly, if at all, and only to check your pitch. The less you use it, the better.

     f. Conduct and sing through the exercise again as musically as possible, observing all dynamic, tempo, phrasing, and articulation markings.

In each sight-singing exercise:

    a. Concentrate on accurate intonation.

    b. Work for steady tempo and rhythmic accuracy.

    c. For musicality, observe all performance markings and the musical style of each example; work for continuity and a clear sense of phrase.

    d. Keep your eyes moving ahead of where you are singing. As your sight reading improves, train your eyes to scan ahead over the next several notes and ultimately over several measures. The farther you are "ahead of yourself," the better your sight reading will be. Train yourself to recognize melodic patterns, such as scale fragments, chord arpeggiations, repetitions, sequences, cadential formulas, and so on. It is both easier and more musical to perform patterns than to merely move from note to note.

    e. Try "silent singing," in which you conduct through an exercise and sing it internally; then check it by singing aloud. This is a very good exercise for improving your "internal ear."

    f. Remember: "Find it, don't fake it." If you are not sure of the next pitch, find it by relating it to a previous pitch either by interval or by relation to the tonic note.

3. *Analysis.* It is a very good idea to analyze the melodies and part music you are performing. Such analyses not only will make it easier to read well but also will increase your awareness of style, musical materials, and techniques. The following points should be noted:

    a. Phrase structure, including cadence placement and types, and periodic structures, if any.

    b. Patterns, such as repetitions, sequences, and returning pitches, which both unify the melody and make it easier to read.

    c. Motivic content.

    d. Structural pitches, the principal notes that give a melody its overall shape and direction.

    e. Harmony. As appropriate, analyze the underlying harmonies implied by the melodic lines, being attentive to the patterns of nonharmonic tones. This will improve your understanding of the relation of harmony to melody, will increase your ability to harmonize melodies quickly and musically, and will make it easier to sing.

Here is a sample analysis of a melody, with structural pitches circled:

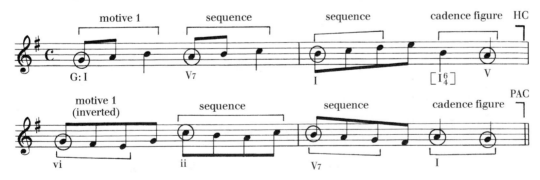

4. This book does not depend on any particular singing system. At the discretion of the teacher, you may use scale-degree numbers, note names, a neutral syllable such as *la*, or the *fixed do* or *movable do* system of *solfège* syllables. We suggest that you initially approach an unfamiliar clef by singing the exercises using note names.

The syllables for the *movable do* system are

The syllables indicated for the chromatic scale as shown here on *C* are those used in the *fixed do* system.

Alternative syllables for minor scales are

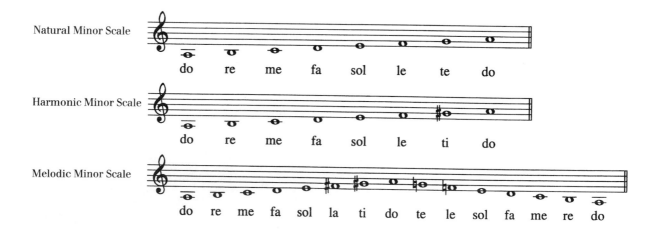

In the *fixed do* system, the syllables always coincide with the letter names of the notes, regardless of key. For example, *C* is always do and *F* is always fa, and so on.

It is also possible to use the *fixed do* system with inflected syllables, as given in the chromatic scale on page x.

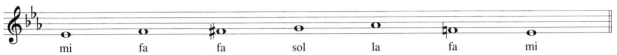

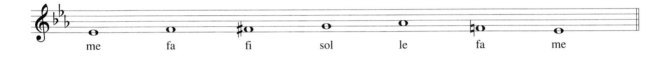

Part I

Common Practice Techniques: Diatonic

1

Rhythm: One- and Two-Pulse Units (Unmetered)

Preliminary Exercises

These exercises introduce one- and two-pulse rhythmic values. They may be performed in a variety of ways, for example, by tapping or clapping the pulse while vocalizing the rhythm.

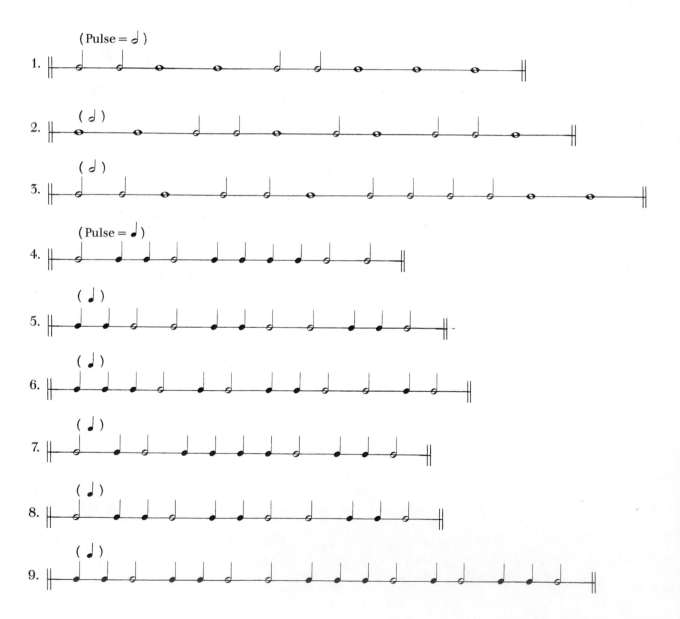

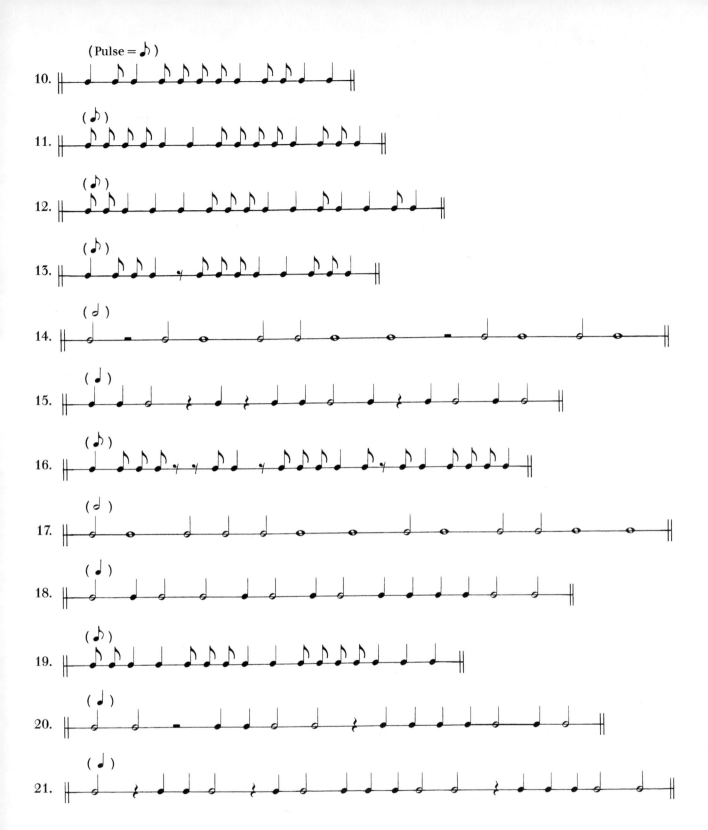

Rhythmic Duets

Rhythmic duets may be performed in the following ways:

1. Separate people vocalizing, tapping, or clapping each part.

2. Each student performing both parts, using some combination of tapping, clapping, or vocalizing.

Pitch: The Major Scale

Preliminary Exercises

These exercises contain only *conjunct* (stepwise) motion. They should be performed by tapping or clapping the pulse while singing the pitches, using scale-degree numbers, a neutral syllable, *fixed do,* or *movable do.*

In all pitch exercises in this book, work for very good intonation. For those without "perfect" (absolute) pitch, give yourself the first pitch, using some instrument, and check your pitch again at the end. Do not use any instrument to help you with difficult passages, as this will result in your not being able to sight sing or internally "picture" the sound. It is often effective and efficient to work with a classmate, alternating singing and listening; this builds both sight-singing and ear-training skills. It may also help you to sing into a tape or disk recorder to check your accuracy.

Perform all exercises only as fast as you can with complete accuracy of pitch and rhythm. As with learning an instrument, speed is not of primary concern at the early stages. Very consciously, keep your eyes scanning ahead of where you are in an exercise, taking in patterns where present.

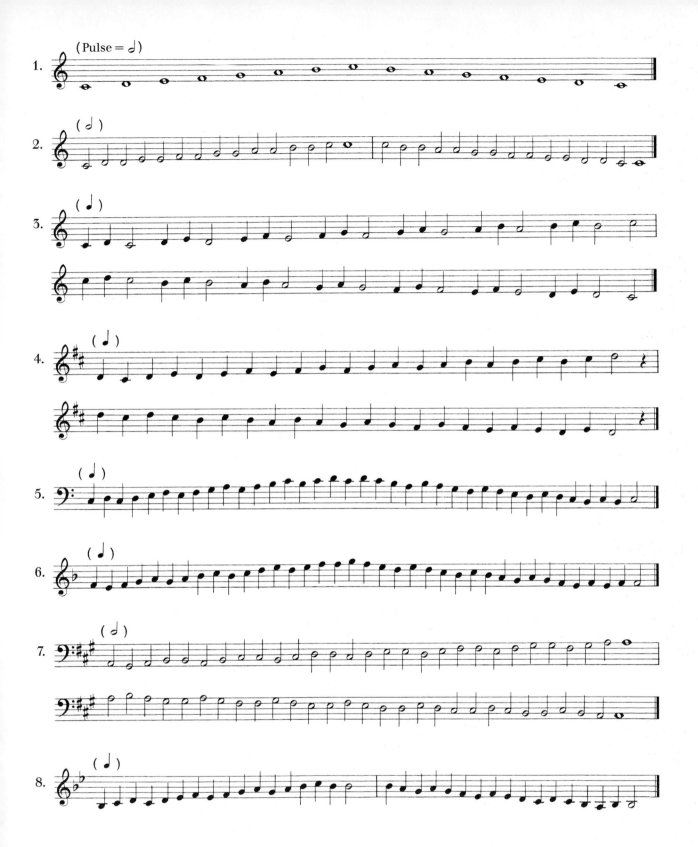

Melodic Exercises

Sing these exercises with great accuracy of rhythm and pitch, and as musically as possible, with good continuity, steady pulse, and attention to the shape of the phrase. For further suggestions for preparing the melodic exercises, see Suggestions to the Student, pp. vii–xi.

19.

20.

21.

22.

Duets

1.

2.

3.

2

Rhythm: Simple Meters

Preliminary Exercises

These exercises introduce simple meters. They should be performed by conducting the meter while vocalizing the rhythm. For conducting patterns, see Suggestions to the Student, pp. vii–xi.

Work hard to make your conducting very clear. Place the beginning of each beat clearly, and work for beats of roughly equal size, weight, and speed. The preparatory beat should be used and practiced; be sure it is the same speed, size, and character as the rest of the exercise. Practice with a classmate, or with a mirror or video recorder. Avoid any large movement of the head or body, and avoid any extraneous gesture that might obscure the beat. Use just one hand to conduct, for now, unless your teacher suggests otherwise.

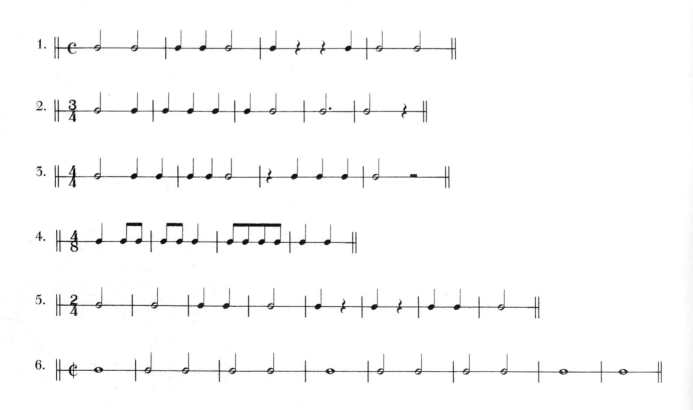

7. 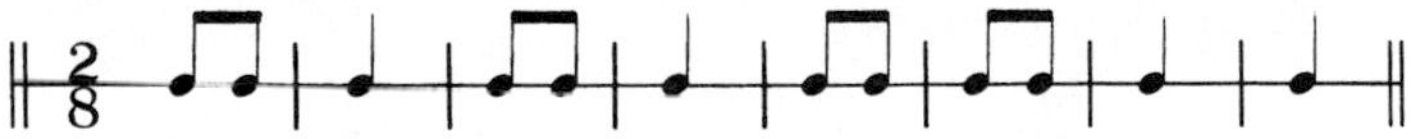

8. 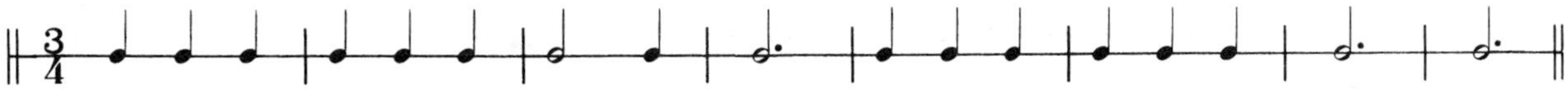

9. 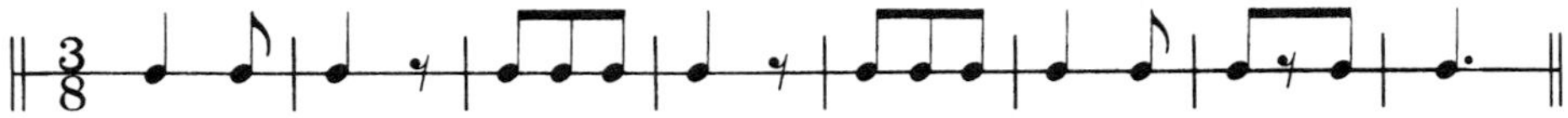

10. 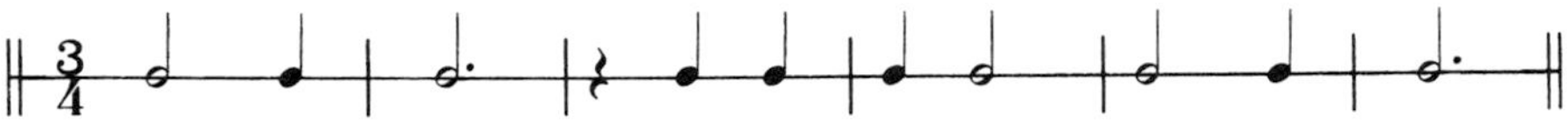

11. 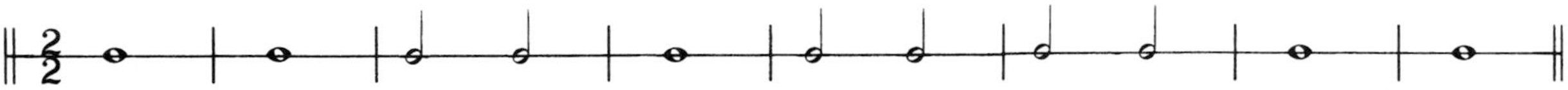

12. 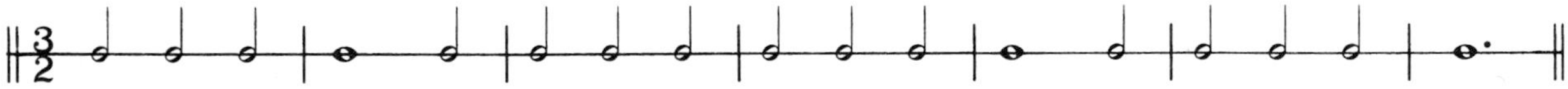

13. 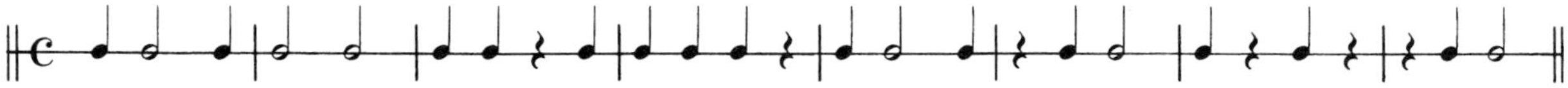

14. 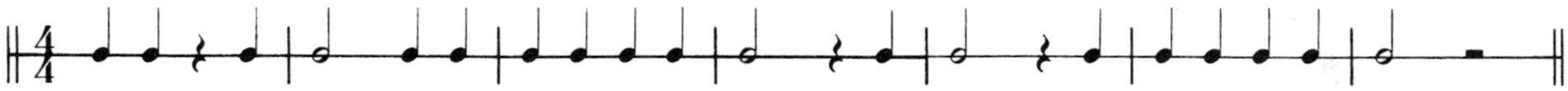

15. 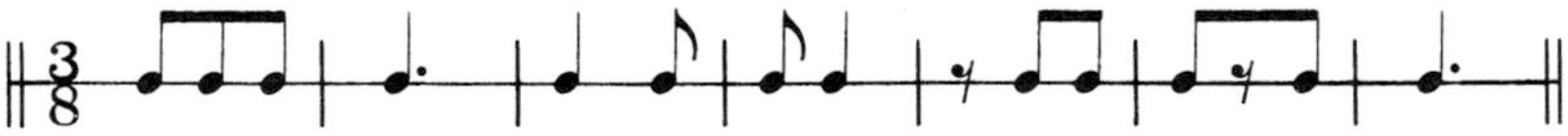

16. 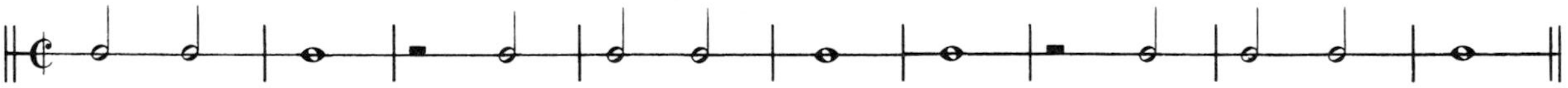

17. 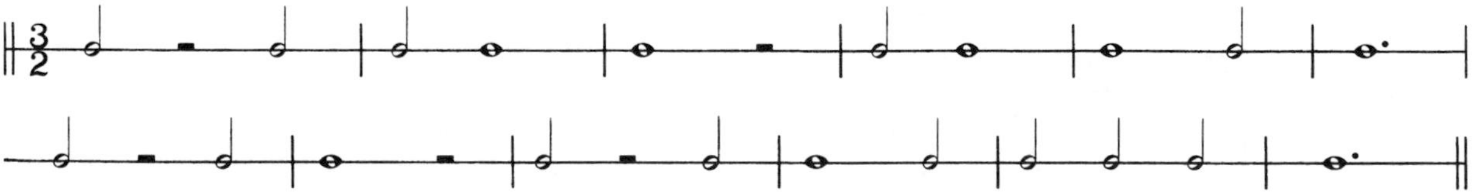

Rhythmic Duets

These duets may be performed in the usual ways: separate people vocalizing, tapping, or clapping each part; or each student performing both parts, using some combination of clapping, tapping, or vocalizing. As always, strive for a simple, clear, even beat, and a completely steady pulse.

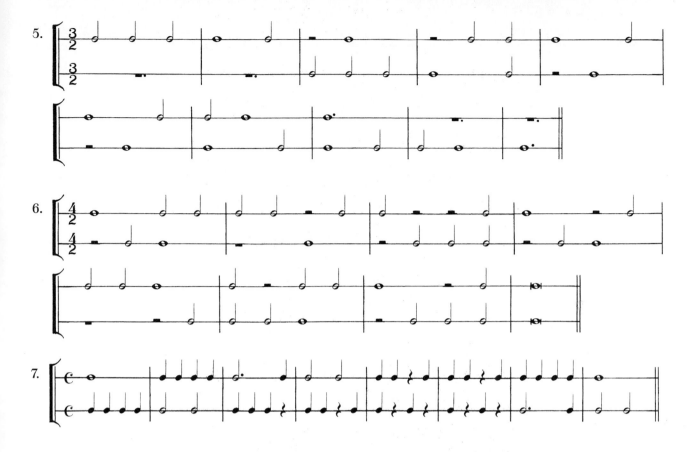

Pitch: Introducing Thirds

Preliminary Exercises

All metered melodies should be conducted as they are being sung.

Sight read and practice these exercises slowly at first, being attentive to accuracy of pitch and rhythm. Be especially careful with the intonation of the leaps; give yourself a starting pitch, and check the pitch again at the end, but use the piano (or any instrument) as little as possible.

Pitch: Introducing Fourths

Preliminary Exercises

Melodies

These and all subsequent melodies should be performed in as musical a manner as possible, with attention to phrasing, dynamics, and tempo markings. Careful analysis of the melodies will be helpful. For procedures for preparation and analysis, see Suggestions to the Student, pp. vii–xi.

As you prepare these melodies, stay conscious of scanning visually ahead of where you are in any exercise, looking for patterns and taking in as much as you can. With these and most subsequent melodies in this book, full editing (tempo, dynamics, phrasing, and articulations) is given. Such markings are as important as the pitches and rhythms, as is the expressive quality and style of each melody. Treat these as music, not "just exercises," as if you were performing them. As always, steadiness of beat and accuracy of pitch are very important. Be sure your conducting patterns (including preparatory beat) are in the same character, dynamic, and tempo as the whole melody. Again, working with a friend, a mirror for conducting, or an audio or video recorder will be helpful.

Duets

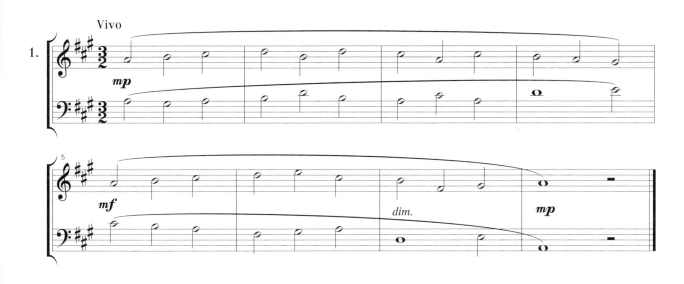

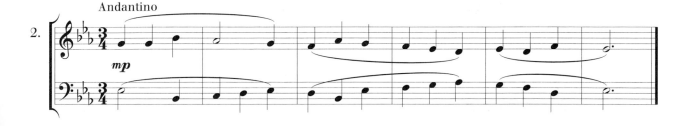

Pitch: Tonic Triad in the Major Mode; Introducing Fifths, Sixths, and Octaves

Preliminary Exercises

As these exercises become more difficult, with more leaps, work on them slowly, with a critical ear for pitch accuracy. Be aware of the "feeling" of an interval in the voice, and also of the importance of "pitch memory," which will help greatly in singing lines involving notes you have already sung. See, for instance, measures 1–2 of the first exercise below. Be equally aware of all patterns of repetition and sequence, and all recurrences of strong scale degrees, such as the tonic and dominant.

Melodies

Canons and Duets

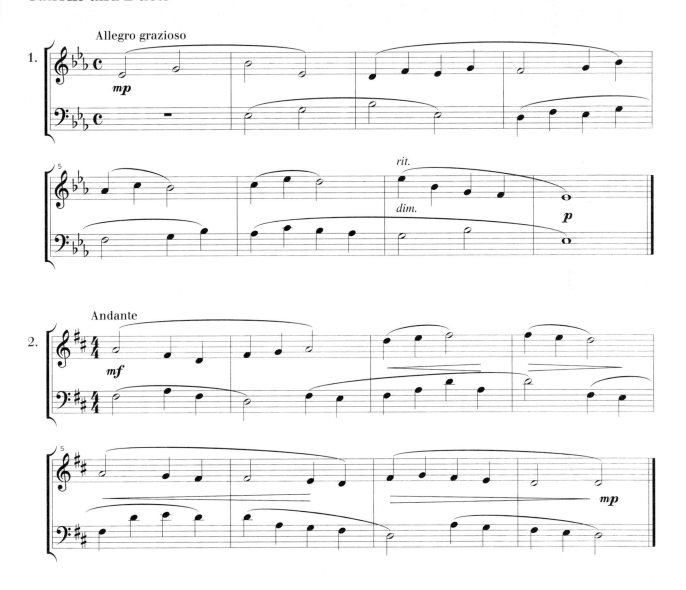

Rhythm: 2:1 Subdivisions of the Beat

Preliminary Exercises

In addition to the usual method of performing these exercises (conducting and vocalizing), it may be useful to tap the subdivisions of the beat.

11. 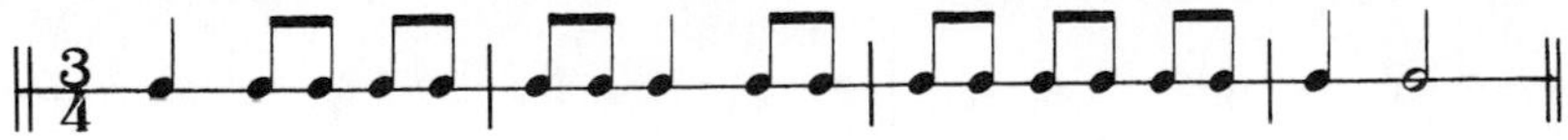

12. 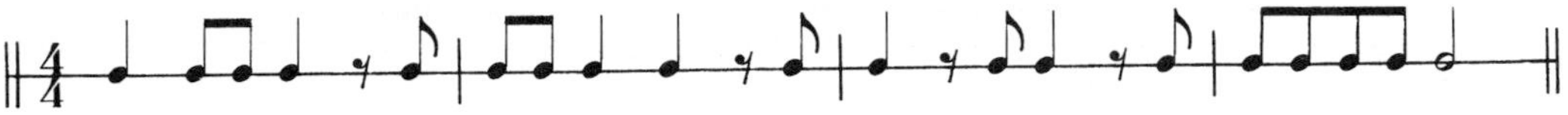

13. 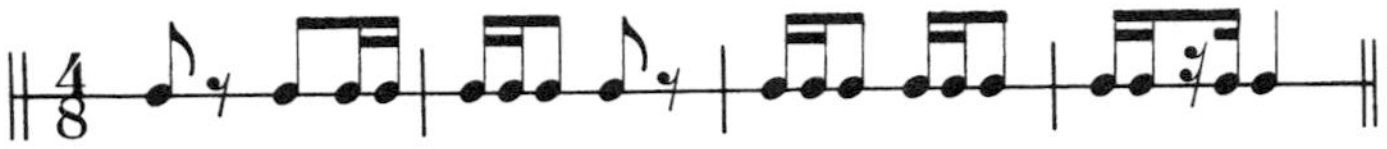

14. 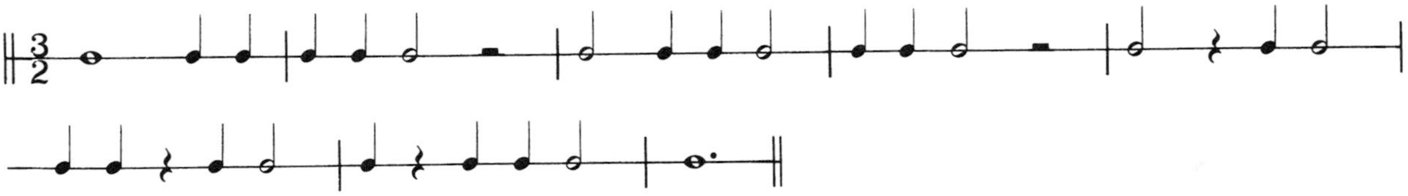

15. 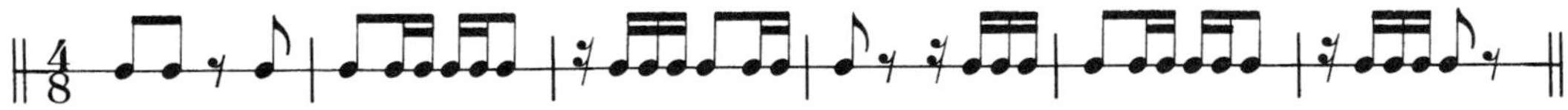

16. 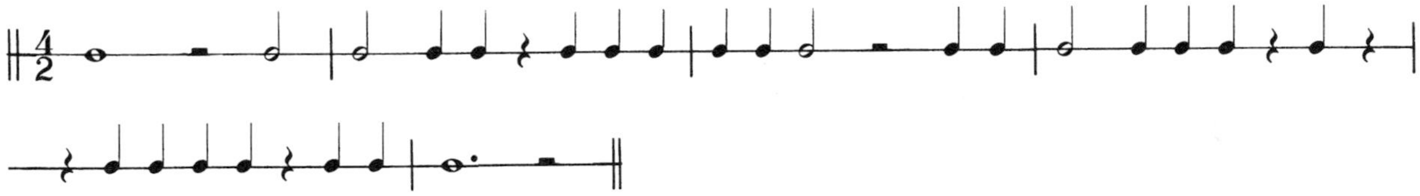

17. 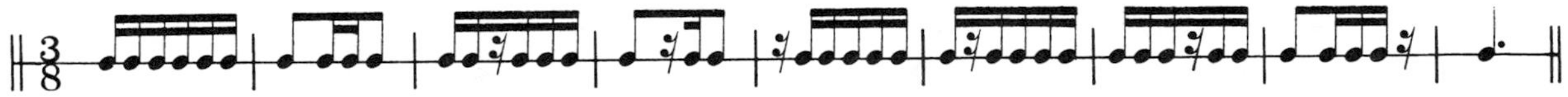

18. 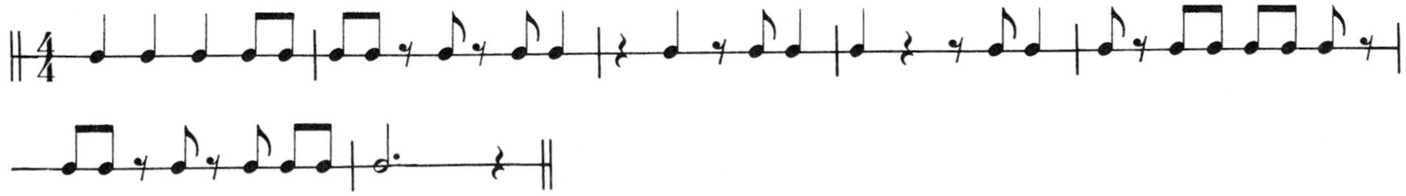

19. 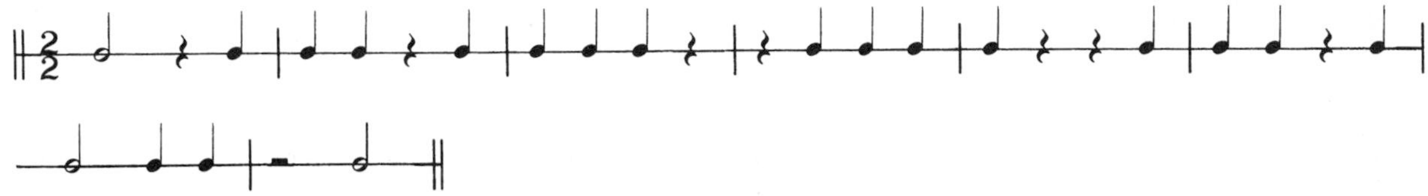

20.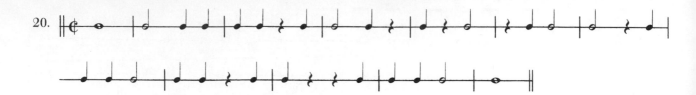

21.

22. Canon

23. Canon

Rhythmic Duets

1. Canon

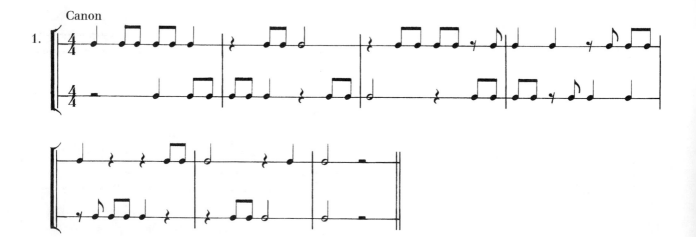

Pitch: I, V, and V₇; Introducing Sevenths

Preliminary Exercises

Careful consideration of the harmonic implications is useful in singing these exercises. Note that the V₇ will not always appear in its complete form melodically. It is possible to analyze the upper three tones of the V₇ as a vii°.

Melodies

As you sight read and practice these melodies, continue to value steadiness, accuracy, and musicality. Sustain through each phrase and observe all cadences. Observe all performance directions with care. Be sure your conducting is in keeping with dynamics, character, and style. Practice, if possible, with a classmate, in front of a mirror, or with a recording device. Keep your eyes scanning as far as possible ahead of your reading, searching for patterns. Check your pitch at the end of each melody.

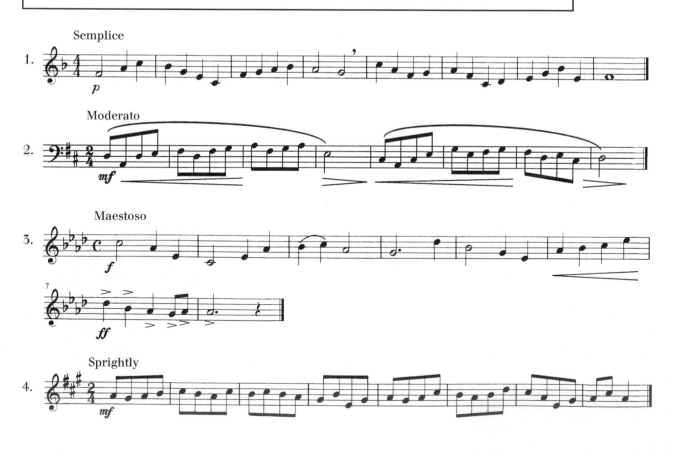

Duets and Canons

Part Music

Sing and Play

Sing the following melody while playing the piano accompaniment. Use solfège syllables
or whatever system you usually employ.

5

Rhythm: Anacruses (Upbeats) and 4:1 Subdivisions of the Beat

Preliminary Exercises

12. 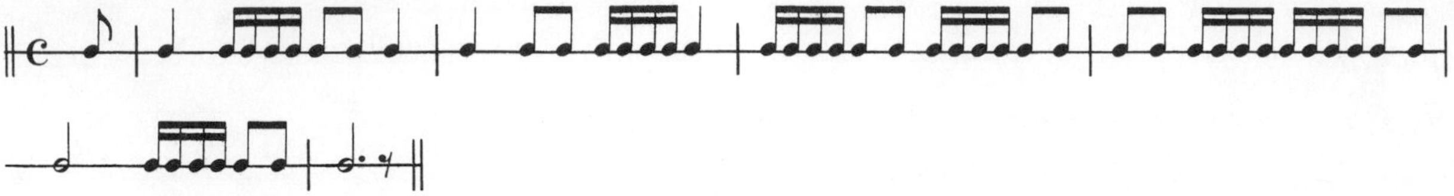

13. 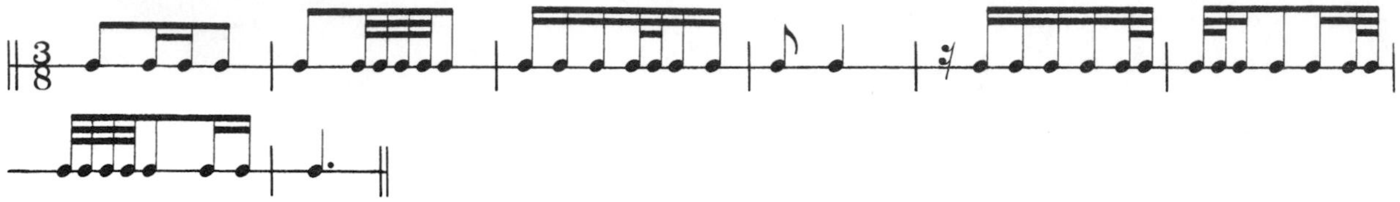

14. 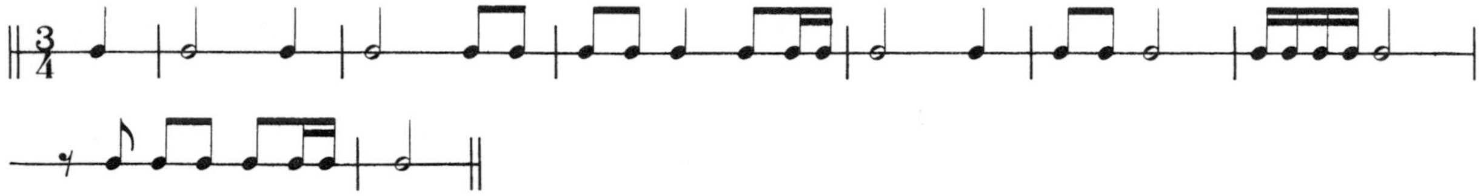

15. 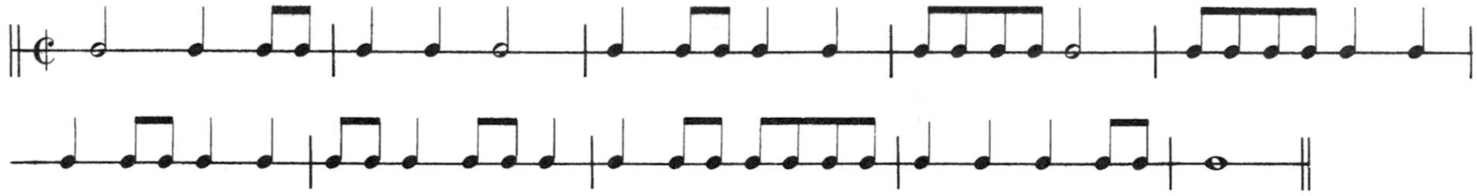

16. 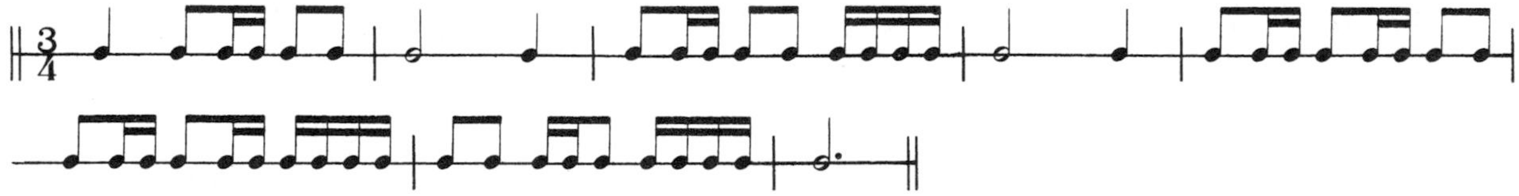

17. 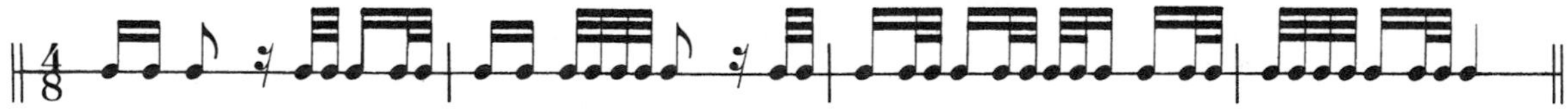

18. 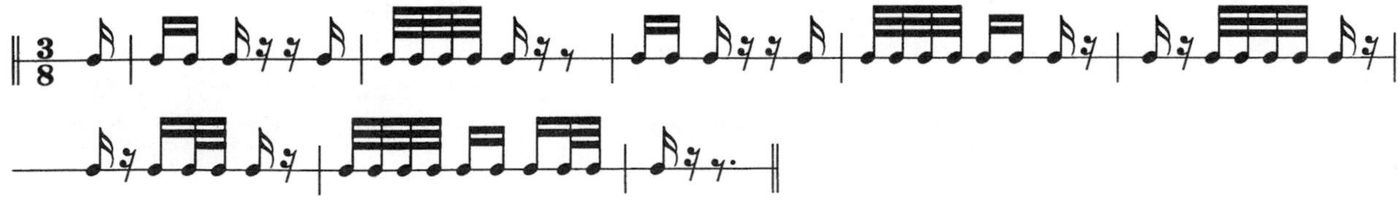

19. 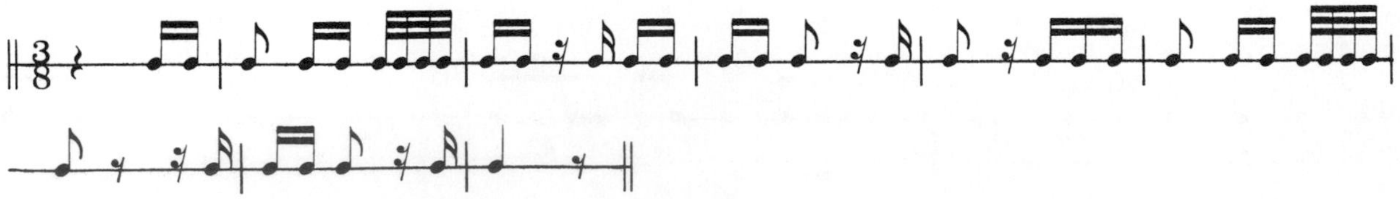

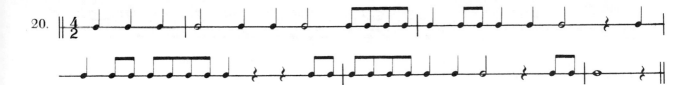

Canons and Duets

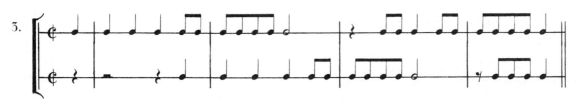

Pitch: I, IV, V, and V_7

Preliminary Exercises

9.

6

10.

11.

12.

13.

7

14.

6

15.

Pitch: Introducing the Alto Clef

Preliminary Exercises

Before singing these exercises, learn the names of the lines and spaces in alto clef. Then perform some of these, conducting and saying the names of the notes. Finally, sing them, using first the note-names and then with solfège syllables. Be sure not to think of the new clef as a transposition of a more familiar clef; this may seem easier at first, but will prevent you from actually learning the new clef.

4.

5.

6.

7.

8.

9.

10.

Melodies

As these melodies are longer, it would be advisable to mark breathing places. Be sure to sustain breath through the phrase, and make the cadences clear in your singing. Conduct and sing with attention to phrasing, character, and dynamics.

Canons and Duets

Part Music

Sing and Play

Sing the following melody while playing the piano accompaniment. Alternatively, the accompaniment may be played by another student, or by the teacher. Use solfège syllables or whatever system you usually employ. This song was originally written for voice and lute. The accompaniment has been adapted for purposes of this exercise.

Dowland, *Awake, sweet love*

6

Rhythm: Dots and Ties

Preliminary Exercises

Canons and Duets

Pitch: Minor Mode

Preliminary Exercises

Compare the major and minor scales. Sing these exercises using either *do* for tonic or *la* for tonic. Pay particular attention to the location of whole steps and half steps and the associated syllable patterns.

Before singing these exercises, analyze the quality of the triads.

18.

19.

20.

21.

22.

23.

24.

25.

26.

27.

Melodies

Duets and Canons

Part Music

7

Music from the Literature

It may be helpful to discuss the historic and stylistic aspects of these brief pieces, and to work toward stylistically appropriate performances. Musicality and expressiveness are as important as accuracy. Texts may be omitted at the discretion of the instructor.

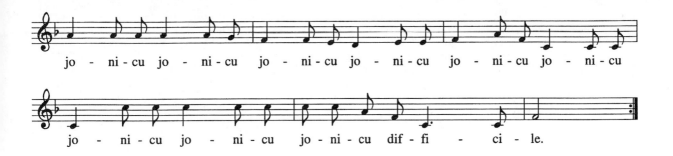

jo - ni - cu jo - ni - cu jo - ni - cu jo - ni - cu jo - ni - cu jo - ni - cu

jo - ni - cu jo - ni - cu jo - ni - cu dif - fi - ci - le.

This is a humorous nonsense Latin text.

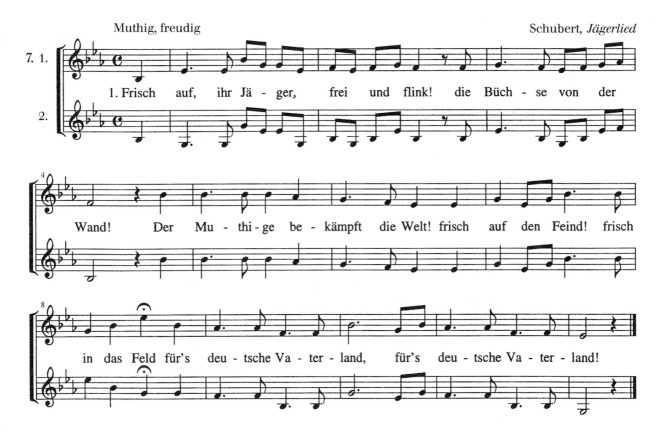

Muthig, freudig

Schubert, *Jägerlied*

7. 1.

2.

1. Frisch auf, ihr Jä - ger, frei und flink! die Büch - se von der

Wand! Der Mu - thi - ge be - kämpft die Welt! frisch auf den Feind! frisch

in das Feld für's deu - tsche Va - ter - land, für's deu - tsche Va - ter - land!

Be quick, you hunters, free and nimble, take the rifle from the wall. The brave conquer
the world. Charge the enemy in the field for the German fatherland!

Henry Harrington, *How Great Is the Pleasure*

8. 1 — How great is the plea - sure, how sweet the de -

2 — How__ great is__ the__ plea - sure, how___ sweet_ the__ de -

3 — Sweet, sweet, how sweet_ the__ de -

light, When friend - ship and mu - sic to - geth - er u - nite.

light,__ When friends in song to - geth - er u - nite.

light,__ When har - mo - ny, sweet har - mo - ny and friend - ship u - nite.

George A. Minor, *Bringing in the Sheaves*

9. Sow - ing in the morn - ing, sow - ing seeds of kind - ness, Sow - ing in the noon - tide

and the dew - y eve; Wait - ing for the har - vest, and the time of reap - ing,

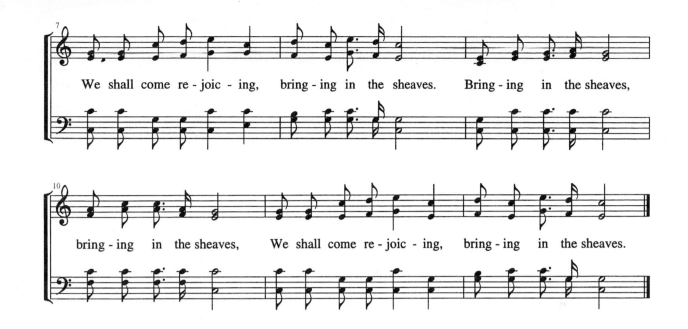

We shall come re - joic - ing, bring - ing in the sheaves. Bring - ing in the sheaves,

bring - ing in the sheaves, We shall come re - joic - ing, bring - ing in the sheaves.

Willy, Prithee Go to Bed

10.

Hey tro lo ly lo ly ly lo ly ly lo ly ly lo ly ly lo ly

Hey ho tro lo ly, tro lo ly ly lo ly ly lo ly

Wil - ly, pri - thee go to bed, For thou wilt have a drow - sy
It is like to be fair weath - er, Coup - le up all thy hounds to-

Hey_____ ho trol - ly, Hey_____ Hey

Welcome, dear, pretty May; to you the birds sing songs of praise.

8

Rhythm: Compound Meter

Preliminary Exercises

These exercises introduce compound meters. The compound duple examples may be
conducted in either two or six, but prefer two in all but the slowest tempos. Conduct compound triple in three or subdivided three, but subdivide only in very slow tempos. Conduct
compound quadruple in four or subdivided four. With these exercises it may be useful to
tap the subdivisions.

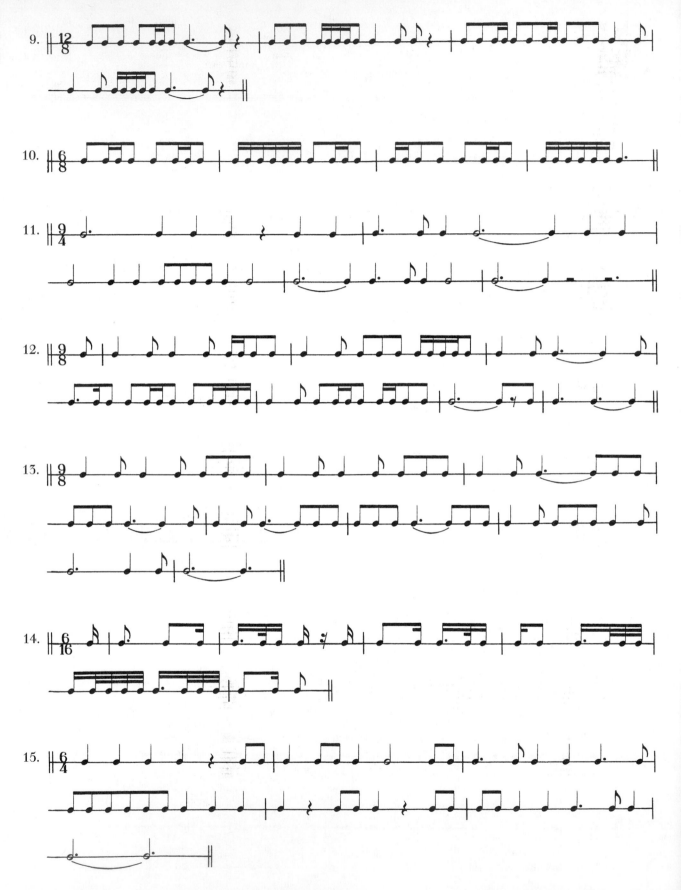

16.

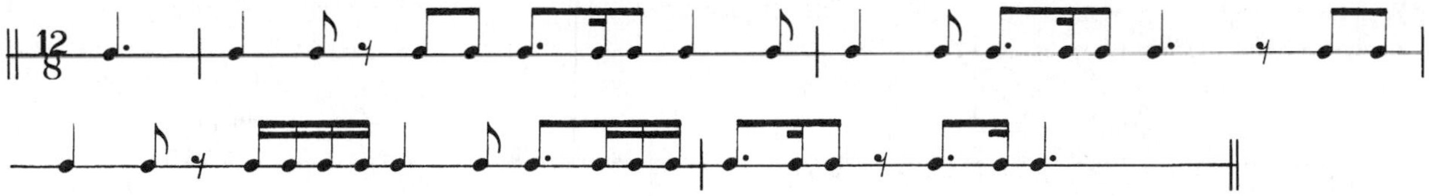

17.

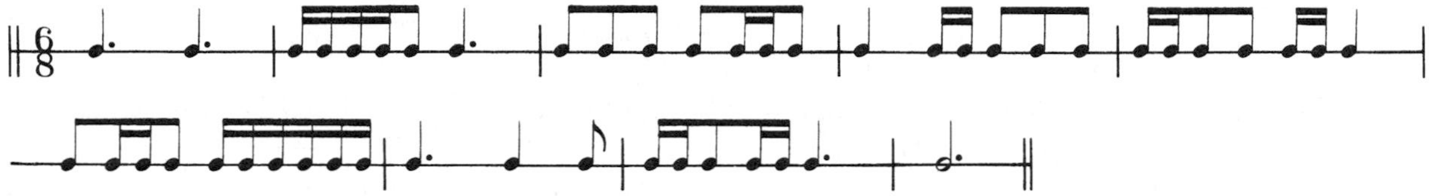

18.

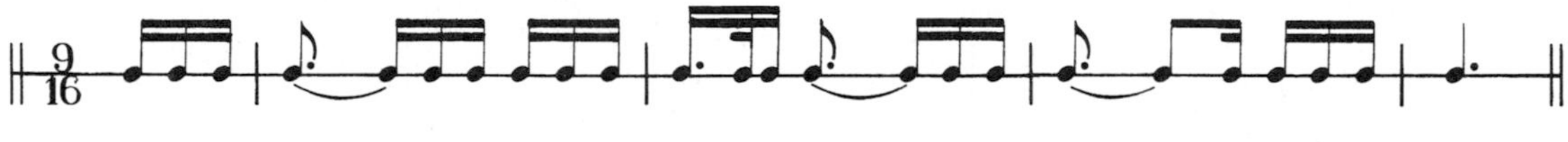

19.

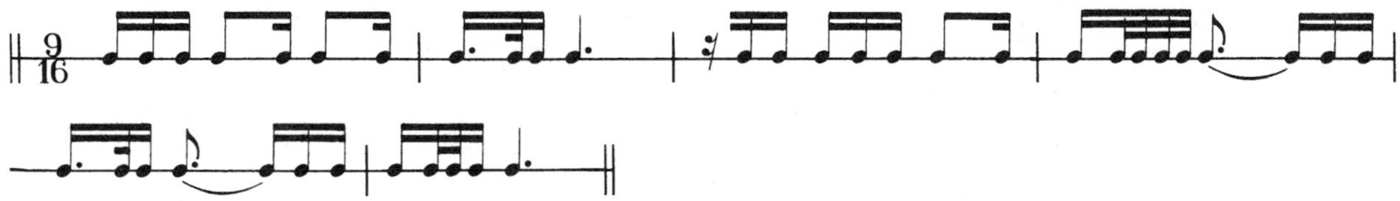

20.

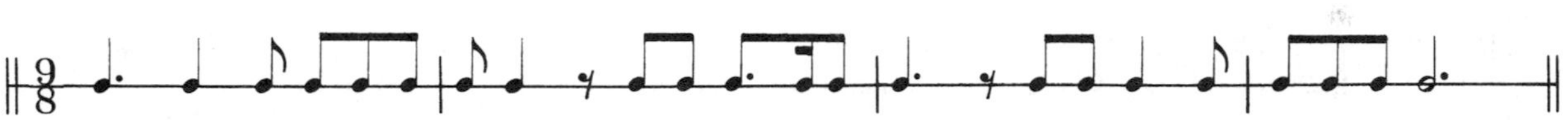

21.

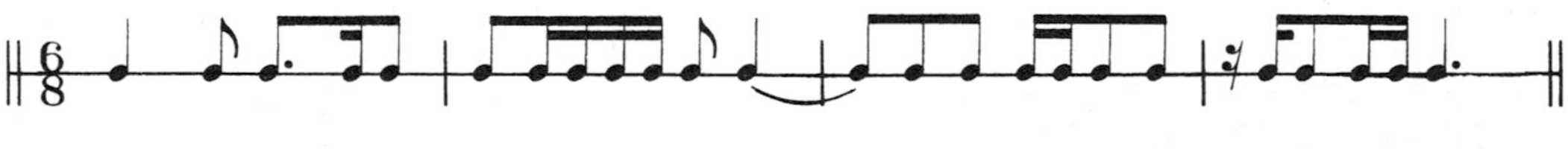

22.

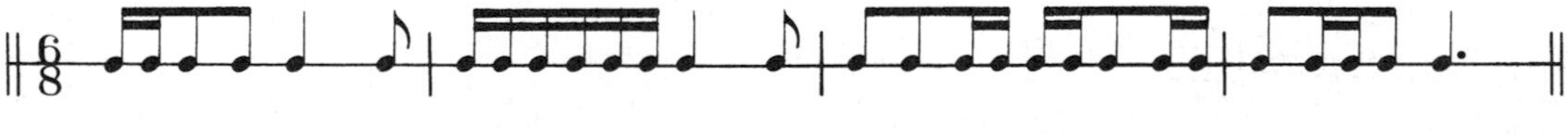

23.

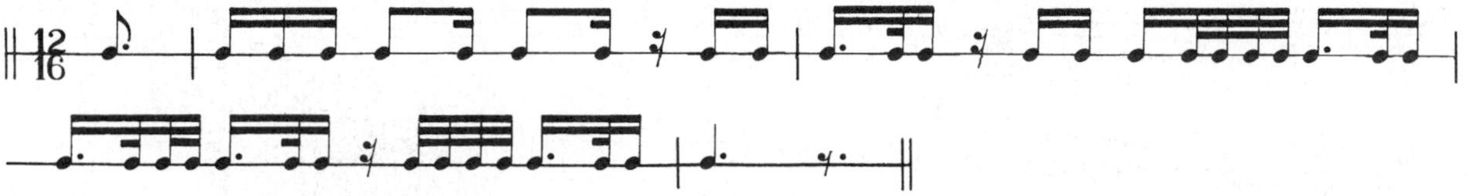

Duets

Pitch: Supertonic Triad

Preliminary Exercises

Pitch: Submediant and Mediant Triads

Preliminary Exercises

Pitch: Tenor Clef

Preliminary Exercises

Learn the names of the lines and spaces first, then perform some or all of these, conducting and saying the names of the notes; then sing them, with note-names; finally, perform them with solfège syllables or whatever system you usually employ. Do not attempt to think of the tenor clef in terms of the transposition of some more familiar clef, as this will prevent you from learning it.

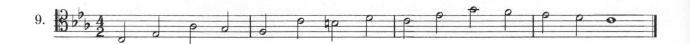

Melodies

Canons and Duets

Part Music

Sing and Play

Sing the following melody while playing the piano accompaniment. Alternatively, the accompaniment may be played by another student, or by the teacher. Use solfège syllables or whatever system you usually employ. This song was originally written for voice and lute. The accompaniment has been adapted for purposes of this exercise.

Dowland, *Now, O now I needs must part*

9

Rhythm: Triplets and Duplets

Preliminary Exercises

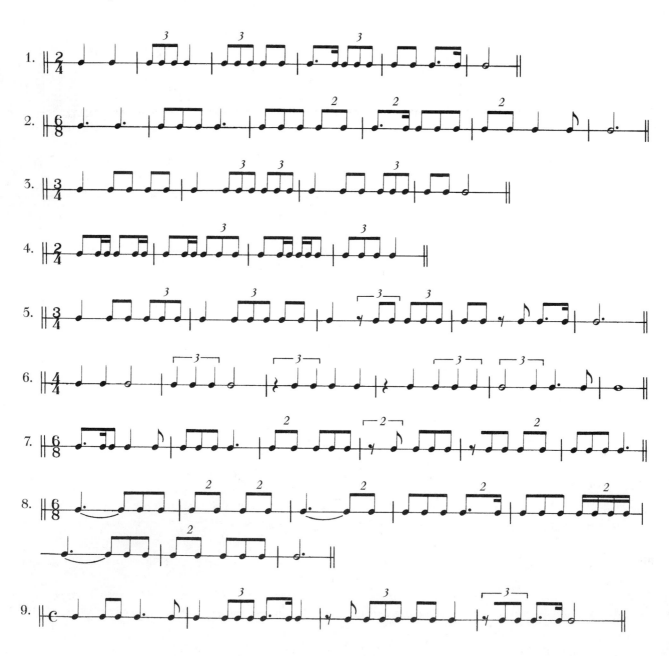

18.

19.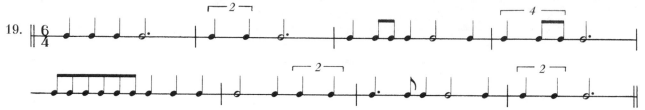

Canons and Duets

1.

2.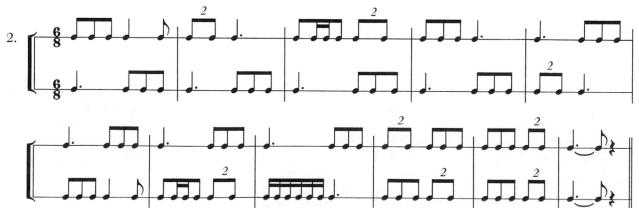

Pitch: Seventh Chords

Preliminary Exercises

6.

7.

8.

9.

10.

11. (image)

12. (image)

Melodies

Smoothly

1.

p

Andante grazioso

6.

Con bravura

7.

Alla marcia

8.

Sing and Play

Sing the following melody while playing the piano accompaniment. Alternatively, the accompaniment may be played by another student, or by the teacher. Use solfège syllables or whatever system you usually employ.

Handel, *Lascia ch'io pianga*

10

Music from the Literature

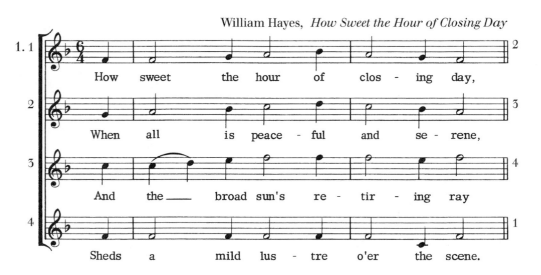

William Hayes, *How Sweet the Hour of Closing Day*

1.1 How sweet the hour of clos - ing day,

2 When all is peace - ful and se - rene,

3 And the ___ broad sun's re - tir - ing ray

4 Sheds a mild lus - tre o'er the scene.

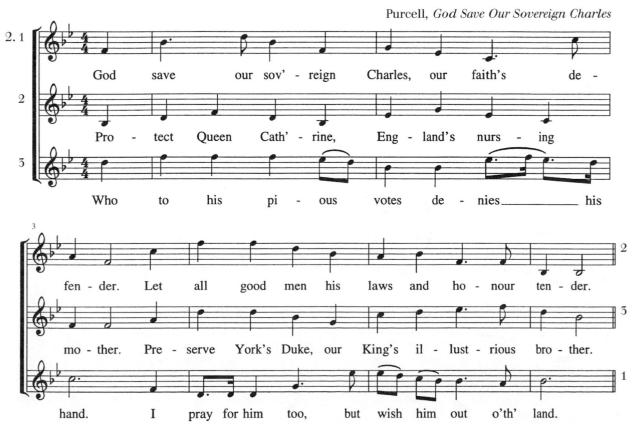

Purcell, *God Save Our Sovereign Charles*

2.1 God save our sov' - reign Charles, our faith's de -

2 Pro - tect Queen Cath' - rine, Eng - land's nurs - ing

3 Who to his pi - ous votes de - nies ___ his

fen - der. Let all good men his laws and ho - nour ten - der.

mo - ther. Pre - serve York's Duke, our King's il - lus - trious bro - ther.

hand. I pray for him too, but wish him out o'th' land.

Andantino

Schubert, *Be Welcome*

5.

Singen wir aus Herzensgrund

6.

Was Gott tut, das ist wohlgetan

7.

Freudig

Schubert, *Mailied*

8.

1. Grü - ner wird die Au, und der Him - mel blau! Schwal - ben keh - ren

wie - der und die Erst - ling's lie - der klei - ner Vö - ge -

The pasture grows greener, and the heavens blue; swallows return, and the songs of the early arrivals twitter through the glade.

ta-ta-ta-ta-ta-ta - too was beat, the ta-ta-ta - ta-ta-ta - too was beat.

_____ and ta-ra-ra-ra-ta-ra-ra-ra - ra-ra-ra-ra-ra is sound-ed on high.

you, let us drink, let us drink till tis day, let, let us drink till tis day.

Allegretto

Haydn, *Vergebliches Glück*

10.

Es ist um - sonst, daß dir das Glück ge - wo - gen ist, wenn

Es ist um - sonst, daß dir das Glück ge - wo - gen

du nicht selbst er - kennst wie sehr du___ glück - lich bist. Es ist um -

ist, wenn du nicht selbst er - kennst, wie sehr du___ glück - lich bist. Es

In vain, when fortune is friendly to you, if you don't know yourself how lucky you are.

Haydn, *Thy Voice O Harmony*

Thomas Morley, *Say, Gentle Nymphs*

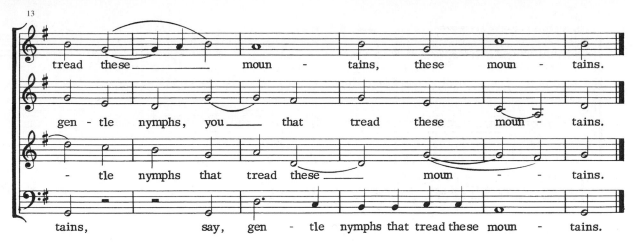

tread these _____ moun - tains, the se moun - tains.

gen - tle nymphs, you _____ that tread these moun - tains.

- tle nymphs that tread these _____ moun - tains.

tains, say, gen - tle nymphs that tread these moun - tains.

Mozart, *Heiterkeit und leichtes Blut*

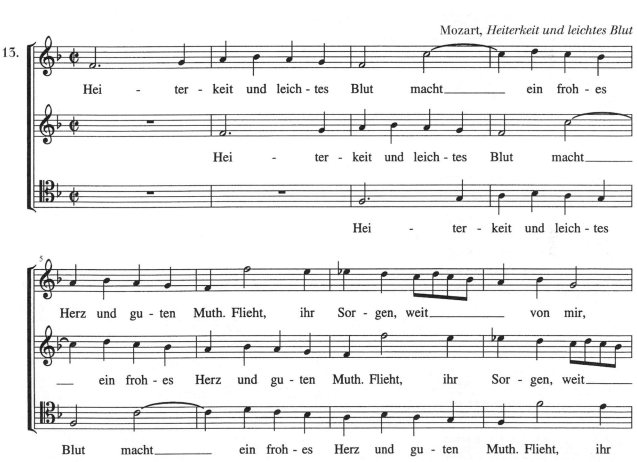

13.

Hei - ter - keit und leich - tes Blut macht _____ ein froh - es

Hei - ter - keit und leich - tes Blut macht_____

Hei - ter - keit und leich - tes

Herz und gu - ten Muth. Flieht, ihr Sor - gen, weit_____ von mir,

___ ein froh - es Herz und gu - ten Muth. Flieht, ihr Sor - gen, weit_____

Blut macht_____ ein froh - es Herz und gu - ten Muth. Flieht, ihr

trübt nicht mei - nes Her - zens Se - - - -

___ von mir, trübt nicht mei - nes Her - zens Se -

Sor - gen, weit_____ von mir, trübt nicht mei - nes Her -

- - lig - keit!

- - lig - keit!

- zens Se - lig - keit!

Happiness and lightheartedness make a merry spirit and a good mood. Fly, cares, away from me, do not disturb my heart's happiness.

Thomas Morley, *Sing We and Chant It*

Sing we and chant it, While love doth grant it,

Sing we and chant it, While love doth grant it,

Sing we and chant it, While love doth grant it,

Sing we and chant it, While love doth grant it,

Sing we and chant it, While love doth grant it,

Mozart, *Auf das Wohl aller Freunde*

Here's to all friends. Let's all live well.

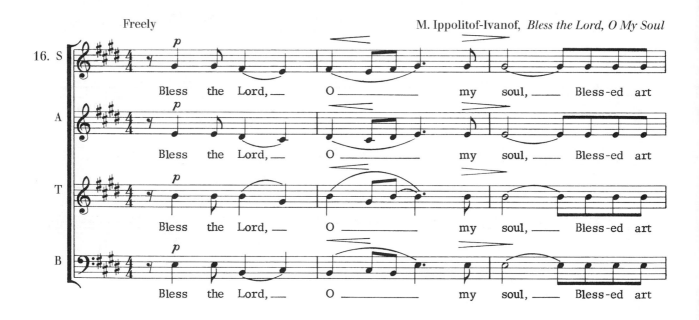

Freely

M. Ippolitof-Ivanof, *Bless the Lord, O My Soul*

16. S
Bless the Lord, — O — my soul, — Bless-ed art

A
Bless the Lord, — O — my soul, — Bless-ed art

T
Bless the Lord, — O — my soul, — Bless-ed art

B
Bless the Lord, — O — my soul, — Bless-ed art

11

Rhythm: Syncopation

Preliminary Exercises

Approach these exercises as you would problems in a piece you are learning. Isolate difficult places; break down beats if necessary into subdivisions; show the location of beats with short vertical lines; practice and drill as slowly as necessary for precision; and conduct all exercises, using a relatively small and precise beat. As always, working with a classmate, metronome, and/or audio recorder can be very helpful.

Canons and Duets

Pitch: Exercises Emphasizing Sixths, Sevenths, and Octaves

Pitch: Other Seventh Chords

Preliminary Exercises

Melodies

Duets and Trios

Part Music

Part **II**

Common Practice Techniques: Chromatic

Pitch: Decorative Chromaticism

Preliminary Exercises

These exercises introduce chromatically altered nonharmonic tones. For the chromatic syllables, see p. x.

In these and all subsequent exercises, absolute precision and clarity of intonation are of great importance. As you sight read and practice, sing only as fast as you can with pitch and rhythmic accuracy. Check your pitch at the end of each exercise and melody. It will be a valuable exercise in both singing and ear training to work on these with a classmate, alternating singing and critiquing. Be sure that the diatonic pitches are in very good tune; if they are, the chromatic notes will be easier to tune. As you sing the first few preliminary exercises, check your intonation every few notes with an instrument.

Melodies

Pitch: Inflected Scale Degrees

Preliminary Exercises

For the solfège syllables for the chromatic scale, see p. x.

Pitch: Scalar Variants in Minor

Preliminary Exercises

Melodies

Read only as fast as complete accuracy allows. Be sure that the diatonic notes are properly tuned; this will improve the intonation of the chromatic notes. Check your pitch at the end. Work with a classmate and critique each other's work with care. Observe all performance markings, and sing and conduct these melodies with a clear sense of phrase. As always, scan ahead to the next few bars or entire phrase. It will be very useful to analyze the implied harmonies, and the nonharmonic tones (identify by category).

Canons and Duets

Part Music

1.

Pitch: Modal Borrowing

Preliminary Exercises

1.

2.

Melodies

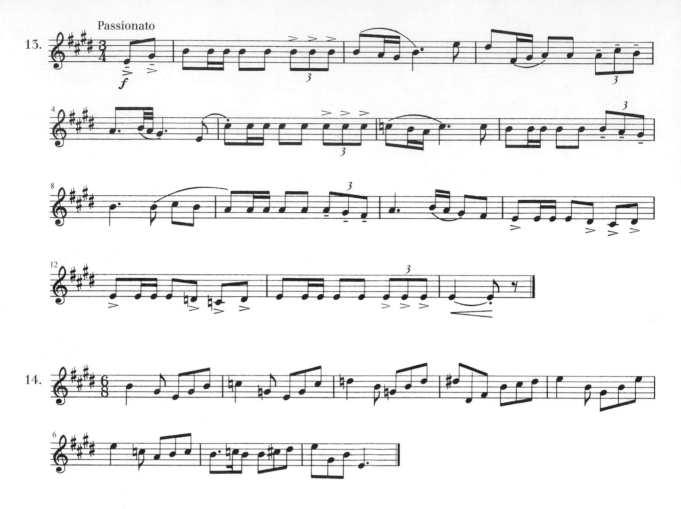

Duets

Part Music

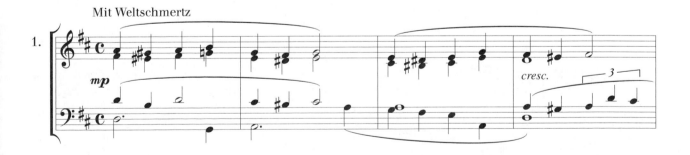

2.

Sing and Play

Sing the following melody while playing the piano accompaniment. Alternatively, the accompaniment may be played by another student, or by the teacher. Use solfège syllables or whatever system you usually employ.

Munter

Mozart, *Das Kinderspiel*

13

Music from the Literature

As with other literature units, research and discuss relevant aspects of music history and literature, style, and performance practice; these matters will provide a very useful context for performance. Musicality and accuracy are equally crucial. The texted exercises may be performed without text, at the direction of the instructor.

1.

Schop, *Werde munter mein Gemüte*

2.

Bach, *Werde munter mein Gemüte*

3.

Schubert, *Der Morgenstern*

Lieblich

Stern der Lie - be, Glanz - ge - bil - de, glü - hend

Star of love, shimmering image, glowing as heaven's bride, you wander through the realm of light, announcing the dawn.

John Smith, *The Silver Swan*

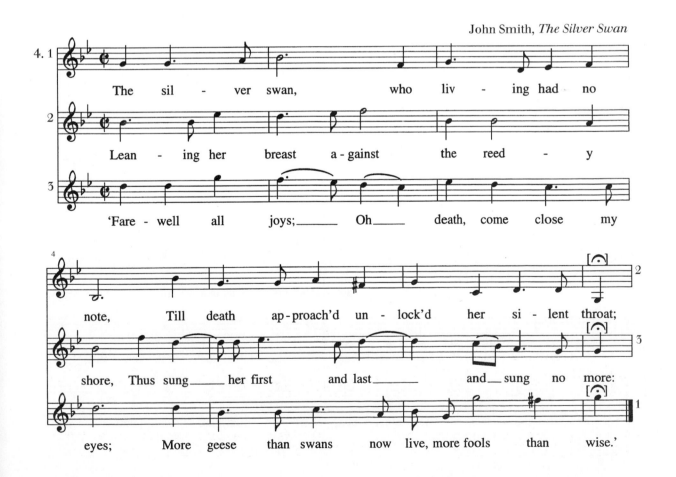

Allegro

5.

Be - fehlt doch drau - ßen still zu schwei - gen, ich muß jetzt mei - nen

Na - men schrei - ben. Be - fehlt doch drau - ßen still zu schwei - gen, ich

Be - fehlt doch drau - ßen still zu schwei - gen, ich

muß jetzt mei - nen Na - men schrei - ben. Be - fehlt doch drau - ßen still zu

muß jetzt mei - nen Na - men schrei - ben, ich muß, ich muß jetzt mei - nen

Ordered by others to be silent, I now must write my name.

14

Pitch: Secondary Dominants

Preliminary Exercises

In preparing these exercises, it will be helpful to first locate and analyze the altered chords.

Melodies

Canons and Duets

Morendo

6.

Sing and Play

Sing the following melody while playing the piano accompaniment. Alternatively, the accompaniment may be played by another student, or by the teacher. Use solfège syllables or whatever system you usually employ. The accompaniments have been adapted for the purposes of this exercise.

15

Pitch: Modulations to Closely Related Keys

Melodies

In preparing these exercises, it will be necessary to determine the keys involved and the point of modulation. At that point, if the *movable do* system is used, the syllables must be changed to conform to the new key.

Canons and Part Music

Allegretto

Sing and Play

Sing the following melody while playing the piano accompaniment. Alternatively, the accompaniment may be played by another student, or by the teacher. Use solfège syllables or whatever system you usually employ.

Haydn, *Liebes Mädchen, hör' mir zu*

16

Rhythm: Quintuple Meters

Preliminary Exercises

To determine the appropriate conducting pattern, analyze these examples to determine the subdivisions of the measure. For conducting patterns, see Suggestions to the Student, pp. vii–xi.

8. 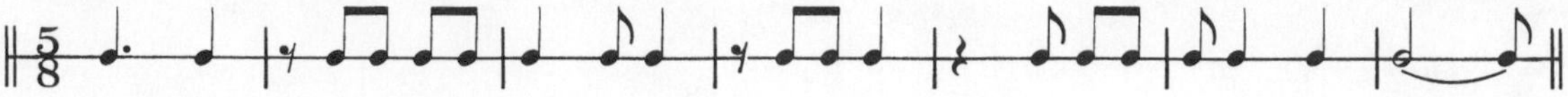

9. 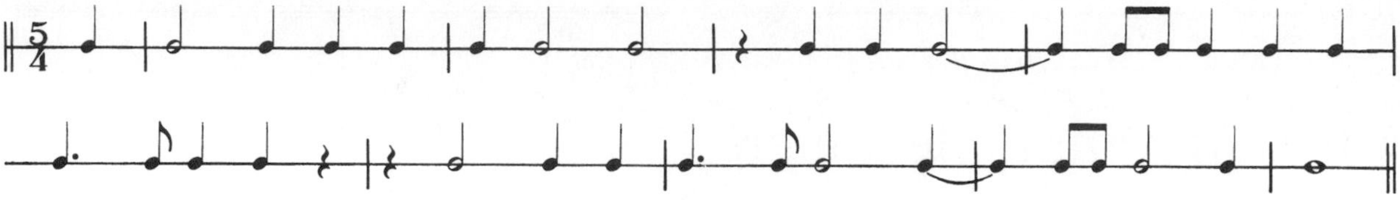

10. 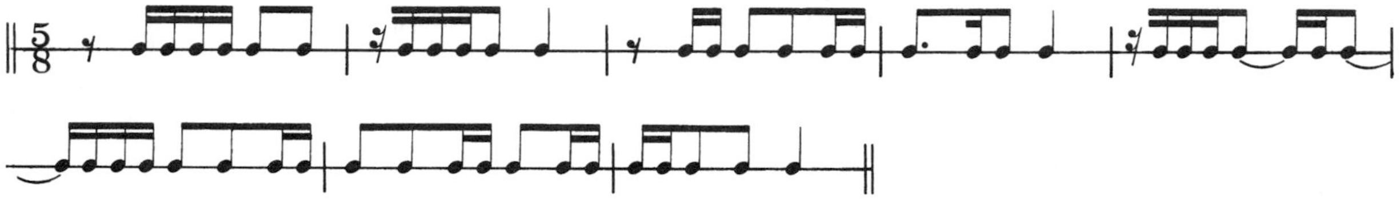

11. 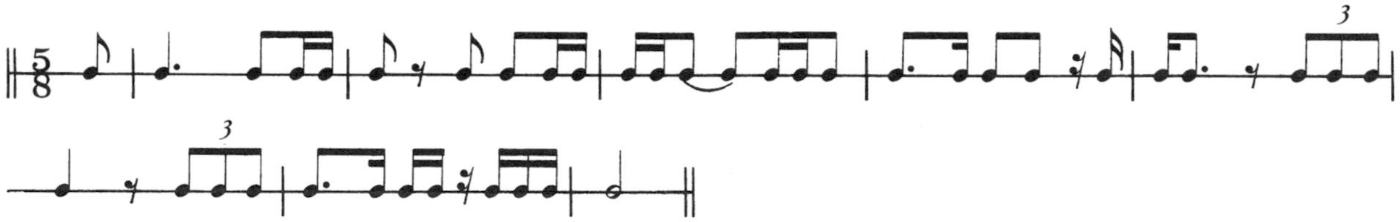

12. 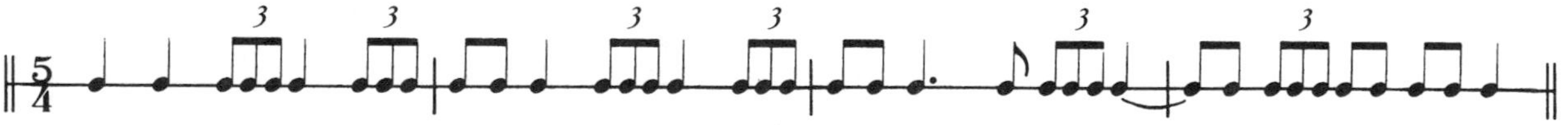

13. 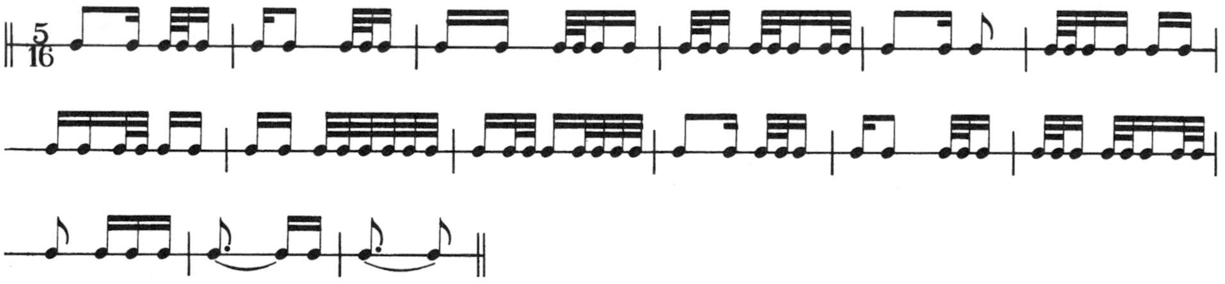

14. 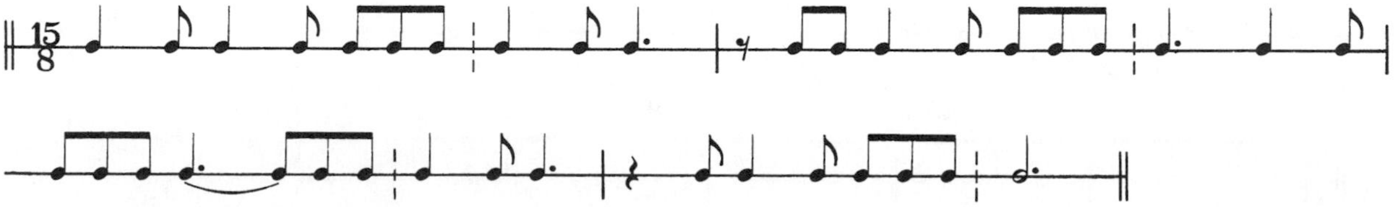

Canons and Duets

Pitch: Chromaticism Implying Altered Chords; Modulation to Distantly Related Keys

Preliminary Exercises

Melodies

As always, analysis of cadences, motives, chords, and nonharmonic tones will be very helpful. Note and identify especially any altered chords, and note the placement and types (categories) of any modulations. Work for a sustained sense of phrase, clear cadences, style-appropriate performance (both singing and conducting), and a high level of accuracy. Try to memorize several measures or an entire phrase ahead of yourself as you sing.

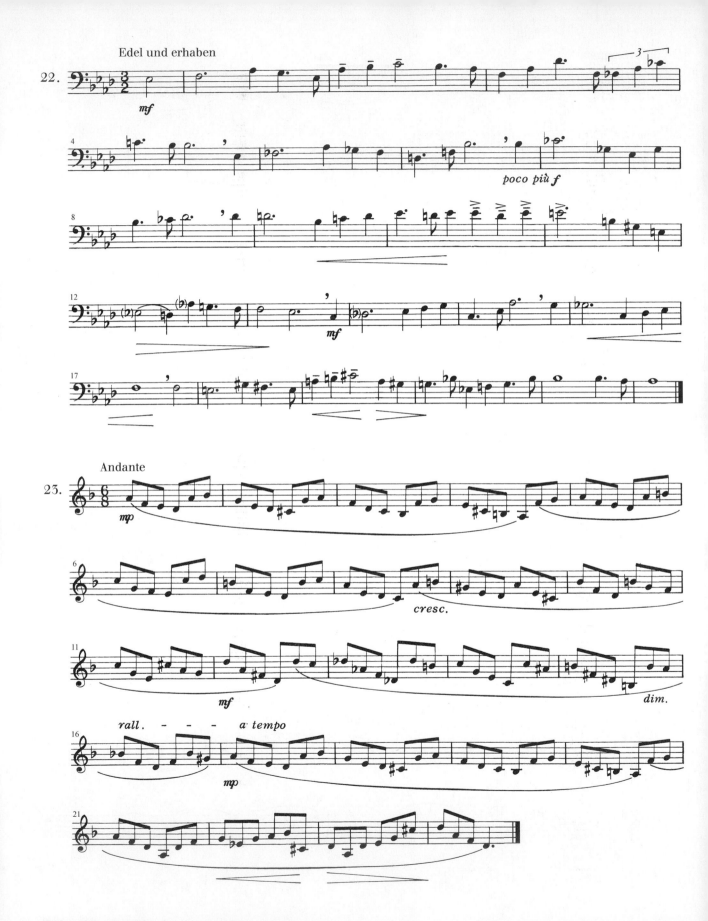

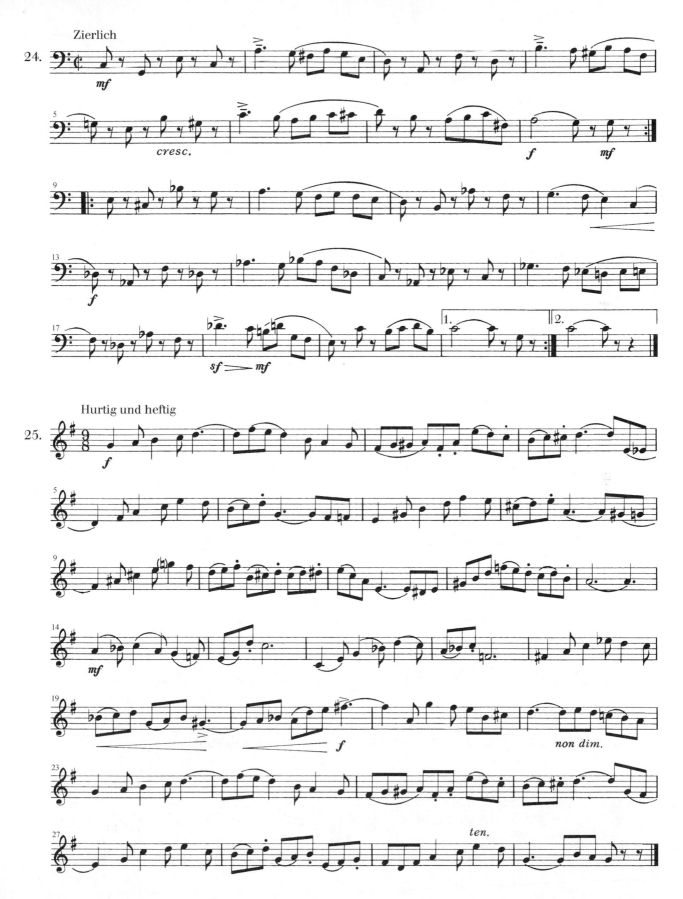

Part Music

Con forza

2.

Breit und feierlich

3.

Sehr ausdrucksvoll

Sing and Play

Andante

Haydn, *An die Freundschaft*

1.

Innig (Con affetto)

Franz, *Widmung*

17

Music from the Literature

1. Beethoven, *Freundschaft*

2. Mozart, *Ave Maria*

A - - ve Ma - ri - a, A - - ve_ Ma - ri - a!

A - - ve, A - - ve_ Ma - ri - a!

A - ve Ma - ri - a, Ma - ri - a, A -

- ve, A - ve Ma - ri - a, A - ve, A - ve!

Here lies Hans with his wife. Hans was a cuckold; what then was his wife?

A singularly wicked wife lives grandly in the world. What a shame that every man deems his wife to be this singular lady.

Haydn, *Hilar an Narziß*

Be by my side, Narcissus, every morning. My large mirror shall be a home for you.

George Hogarth, *Sound the Clarion!*

Haydn, *Auf einen adeligen Dummkopf*

That's what I call a nobleman: his great-great-great ancestor was older by one day than any of our ancestors.

ten - go sem - - pre de - si - o d'es - ser vi -

ci - no, vi - ci - no a te,___ vi - ci - no a___

te, a te. Ca - ro bell' i - dol, i - dol mi - o,

non ti scor - dar___ non ti scor - dar di me, ah___

no, non ti scor - dar___ di___ me!_____ Ca -

- - ro bell' i - - dol mi - o non ti scor -

dar,___ non___ ti___ scor - dar di me, ah, no, non ti scor -

dar di me!

Dear, beautiful idol of mine, do not forget me.

glos - - - es, hark her love too dis - clo - -
wan - ton glos - - es, hark her love too dis -
- - es too dis - clos - - es, Hark
- clos - - - - - - - es, Hark her love
her love too dis - clos - es too dis - clos - es. Where the sweet - es.
too dis - clos - es too dis - clos - - es. - es.

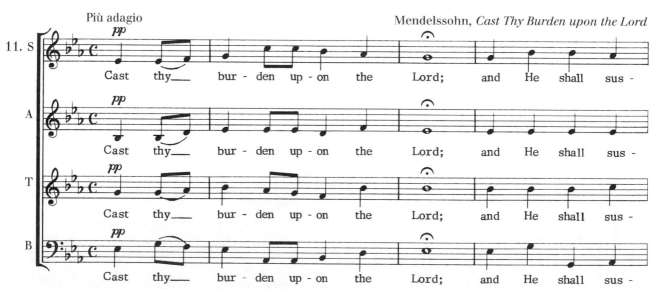

Più adagio

Mendelssohn, *Cast Thy Burden upon the Lord*

11. S Cast thy___ bur - den up - on the Lord; and He shall sus -
A Cast thy___ bur - den up - on the Lord; and He shall sus -
T Cast thy___ bur - den up - on the Lord; and He shall sus -
B Cast thy___ bur - den up - on the Lord; and He shall sus -

At one time, C clefs other than Alto clef and Tenor clef were commonly used. Mezzo-soprano clef locates middle C on the second line; Soprano clef locates middle C on the first line. For practice in reading these clefs, here is a Bach chorale with its original clefs.

J. S. Bach, *Was Gott thut, das ist wohlgethan*

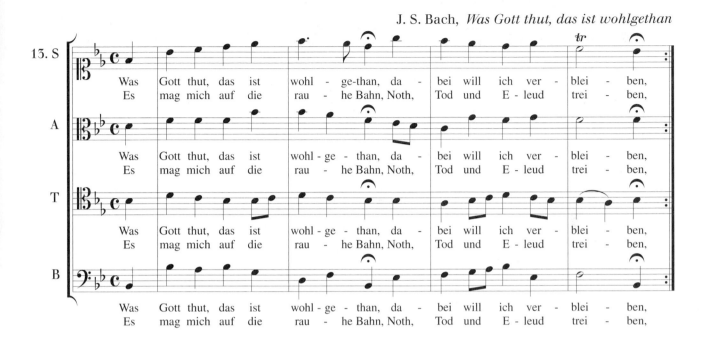

What God does is good; in this opinion I will persist.
Even if my lot is a rough one, (even if it is) need, death, and misery.
God will hold me like a father in his arms—therefore I will let Him rule.

J. S. Bach, *Break Forth, O Beauteous, Heavenly Light*

14. S

Break forth, O beau-teous, heav'n-ly light. And ush - er in the

A

Break forth, O beau-teous, heav'n-ly light, And ush - er in the

T

Break forth, O beau-teous, heav'n-ly light, And ush - er in the

B

Break forth, O beau - teous, heav'n-ly light, And ush - er in the

morn - ing; Ye shep - herds, shrink not with af - fright, But

morn - ing; Ye shep - herds, shrink not with af - fright, But

morn - ing; Ye shep - herds, shrink not with af - fright, But

morn - ing; Ye shep - herds, shrink not with af - fright, But

hear the an - gel's warn - ing. This Child, now weak in

hear the an - gel's warn - ing. This Child, now weak in

hear the an - gel's warn - ing. This Child, now weak in

hear the an - gel's warn - ing. This Child, now weak in

J. S. Bach, *Thee with Tender Care*

Thee: Thus I shall not per - ish, But with Thee a - bide for -

Thee: Thus I shall not per - ish, But with Thee a - bide for -

Thee: Thus I shall not per - ish, But with Thee a - bide for -

Thee: Thus I shall not per - ish, But with Thee a - bide for -

ev - er, Joy - ful - ly, peace-ful - ly, Where life end-eth nev - er.

ev - er, Joy - ful - ly, peace-ful - ly, Where life end-eth nev - er.

ev - er, Joy - ful - ly, peace-ful - ly, Where life end-eth nev - er.

ev - er, Joy - ful - ly, peace-ful - ly, Where life end-eth nev - er.

Etwas langsam   Brahms, *In stiller Nacht*

16. Soprano

In stil - ler Nacht, zur er - sten Wacht, ein Stimm be - gunnt zu

Alto

In stil - ler Nacht, zur er - sten Wacht, ein Stimm be - gunnt zu

Tenor

In stil - ler Nacht, zur er - sten Wacht, ein Stimm be - gunnt zu

Bass

In stil - ler Nacht, zur er - sten Wacht, zu

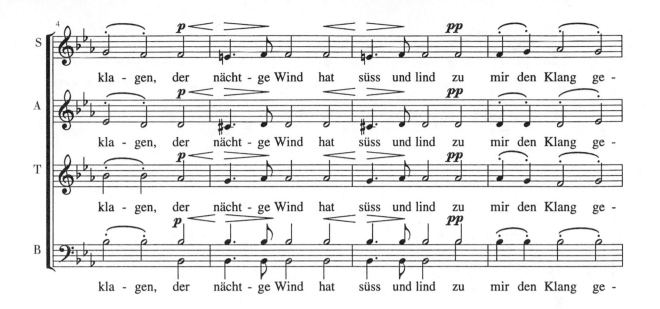

klagen, der nächt-ge Wind hat süss und lind zu mir den Klang ge-

tragen; von her-bem Leid und Trau-rig-keit ist mir das Herz zer-

flos - sen, die Blü - me - lein, mit Trä - nen rein hab ich sie all be - gos - sen.

flos - sen, die Blü - me - lein, mit Trä - nen rein hab ich sie all be - gos - sen.

flos - sen, die Blü - me - lein, mit Trä - nen rein hab ich sie all be - gos - sen.

flos - sen, die Blü - me - lein, mit Trä - nen rein hab ich sie all be - gos - sen.

In the still of night, at the first watch, a voice began to lament; the night wind brought me the sweet, soft sound. With bitter pain and sadness my heart was overflowing; I watered the little flowers with my pure tears.

He was crucified for us under Pontius Pilate, suffered, and was buried.

. . . for thy great glory.

Mendelssohn, *Elijah,* "Thanks Be to God"

Schubert, *Mass in E♭ Major*, "Benedictus"

Blessed is he who cometh in the name of The Lord.

It is enough! Lord, if it please Thee to make me depart. My Jesus comes. Now good night, oh world. I go to my heavenly home. I surely go there with joy. My great sorrow remains below. It is enough, it is enough!

J. S. Bach, *Chorale*, "Christus, der uns selig macht"

22.

Christ-us, der uns se - lig macht, kein Bös's hat be - gan - gen,

der ward für uns in der Nacht als ein Dieb ge - fan - gen,

ge - führt vor gott - lo - se Leut' und fälsch - lich ver - kla - get,

Christ, who makes us blessed, who has done no wrong, who was taken for us like a thief in the night, led before a Godless people and falsely accused, laughed at, scorned and spit upon, according to the Scriptures.

Gluck, *Orfeo,* "Le Porte Stridano"

Let the doors, squealing on black hinges, surely and freely give passage to the victor!

Wagner, *Chorus of the Elder Pilgrims*

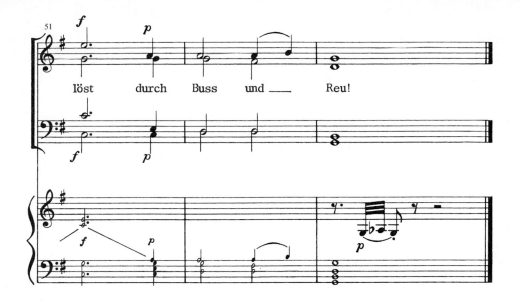

löst   durch   Buss   und ___   Reu!

I make my pilgrimage to Thee
O God, Who art the pilgrim's hope!
Praised be the Virgin, sweet and pure!
Be gracious to the pilgrimage.

The burden of sin heavily weighs me down;
I can no longer bear it.
Thus I wish no rest
    and gladly choose toil and pain.
At the high festival of Grace
    I shall humbly pay for my guilt.
Blest be he who is true to his faith,
He shall be saved through penance.

Brahms, *Waldesnacht*

26.

Wal - des nacht du wun - der küh - le, die ich tau - send - ma - le

Thou wondrously cool forest night,
  I greet you a thousand times.
After the loudness of the troubled world,
  how sweet is your rustling.
Dreamily I lay my tired limbs
  softly on the mossy ground.
And it seems that I have once again
  become free of all my troubles.

Mozart, *Ave verum corpus*

Hail holy body, born of The Virgin Mary, truly having suffered, sacrificed on the cross for man, whose pierced side flowed with water and blood: be for us a foretaste in the trial of death.

Glory to God in the highest.

Part III

Twentieth-Century Techniques

18

Rhythm: Irregular Meters

Preliminary Exercises

> Analyze and mark the subdivision of each measure to determine the proper conducting pattern. Will the same pattern apply to every bar? Prefer a slower to a faster beat in general (that is, generally conduct quintuple meters in two, and septuple meters in three, except when tempos are very slow). Perform only as fast as rhythmic precision allows. Use a relatively small, very precise conducting pattern, with a clear *ictus* (placement of beat arrival).

Pitch: Diatonic Modes

Preliminary Exercises

In singing modal music, one may determine the syllable name for the tonic note from the key signature. For example, *mi* would be the name of the tonic note in Phrygian mode, and *sol* would be the name of the tonic note in Mixolydian mode.

Pitch: Changing Clefs

Melodies with Changing Clefs

Melodies

Part Music

With motion

Shalom

1.

Sha - lom, sha - lom, ___ sha - lom, ___ sha -

Sha - lom, ___ sha - lom, ___ sha - lom, ___ sha -

Sha - lom, ___ sha - lom, sha - lom, ___

Sha - lom, sha - lom, sha - lom, ___ sha -

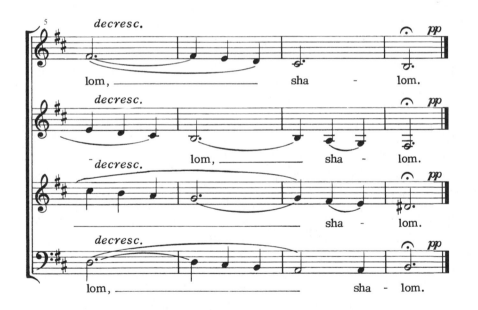

decresc. ___ *pp*

lom, ___ sha - lom.

decresc. ___ *pp*

lom, ___ sha - lom.

decresc. ___ *pp*

sha - lom.

decresc. ___ *pp*

lom, ___ sha - lom.

Peace.

Smoothly

Dona nobis pacem

Give us peace.

Accompanied Canon
Slowly and smoothly

19

Rhythm: Changing Meters

Preliminary Exercises

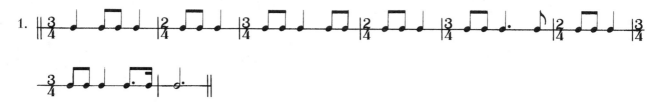

1.

2.

3.

4.

5.

Pitch: Pandiatonicism

Religioso

7.

The Place Where We Meet

13. The place where we meet to seek the high - est is

The place where we meet to seek the high - est is

The place where we meet to seek the high - est is

The place where we meet to seek the high - est is

14.

Praise God

17.

20

Rhythm: Syncopation Including Irregular and Mixed Meters

Preliminary Exercises

6.

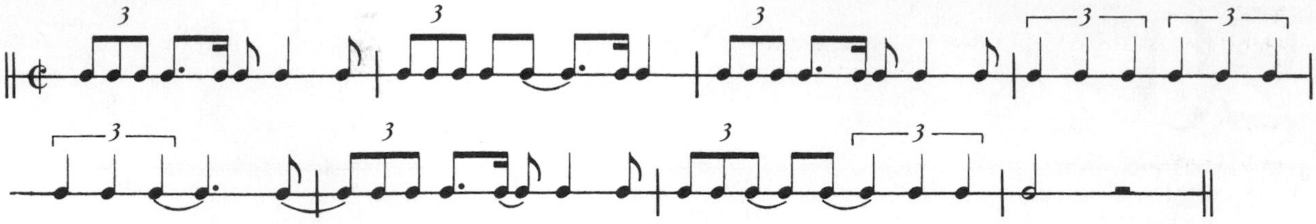

7.

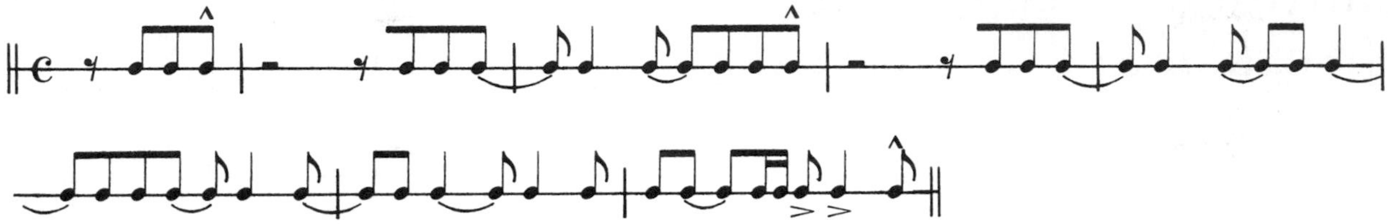

8.

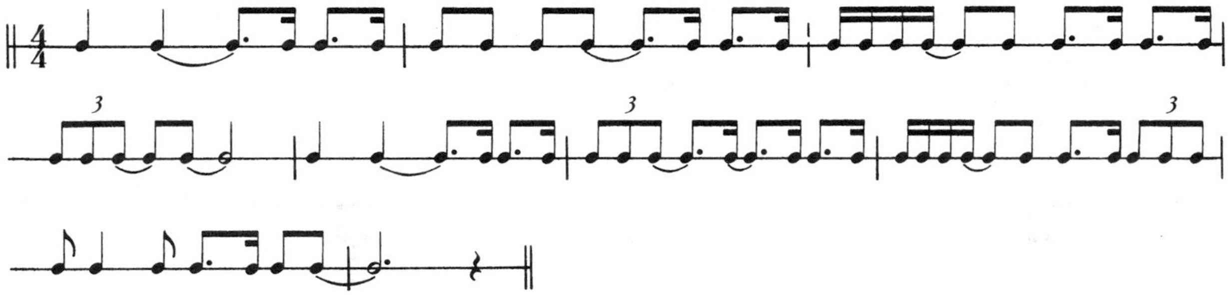

9.

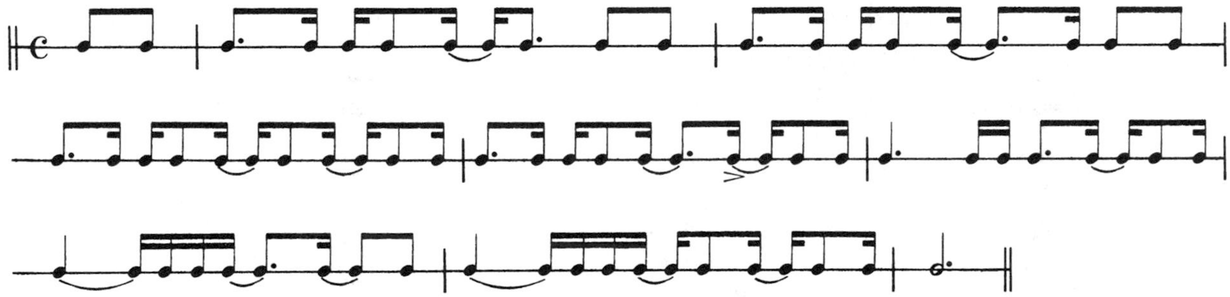

10.

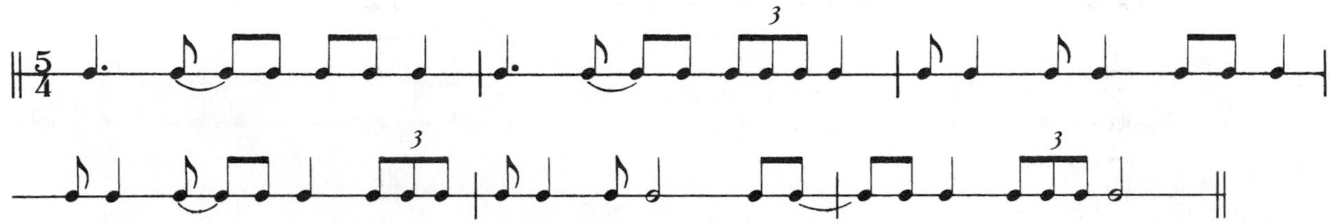

Pitch: Extended and Altered Tertian Harmony

Preliminary Exercises

Analyzing these exercises for harmonic content and melodic pattern before singing them will be helpful.

Possible strategies for hearing and singing are:

1. Using *fixed do* without inflected syllables.

2. Using *fixed do* with inflected syllables.

3. Using *movable do* locally for rapidly moving chordal or scalar patterns, as in exercises 8 ff.

4. Using a neutral syllable.

Melodies

Slowly

Shalom

17.

Sha - lom,   Sha - lom (etc.)

(simile)

poco accel.

poco rit.

Tempo I

Performance directions: Very distant and pure tone; blend and balance with care; no vibrato; observe dynamics carefully. All attacks and releases cued by the conductor.

Note and rest values:

○ 𝄻 = very long   ♩ ︿ = long   ♩ ⌢ = shorter   ♪ , = shortest

21

Pitch: Exotic Scales

Preliminary Exercises

Analyzing these exercises for tonal center (if any), scalar types, and melodic patterns will be helpful.

Melodies

Analyze each melody first as to tonal center, scale, and interval patterns within the scale and in relation to the tonal center.

Innocente

Semplice

6.

Leggiero

7.

Semplice

8.

Lent

9.

Duets

22

Rhythm: Complex Divisions of the Beat

Preliminary Exercises

7.

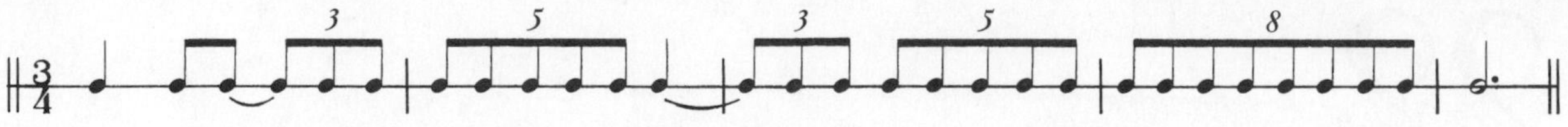

8.

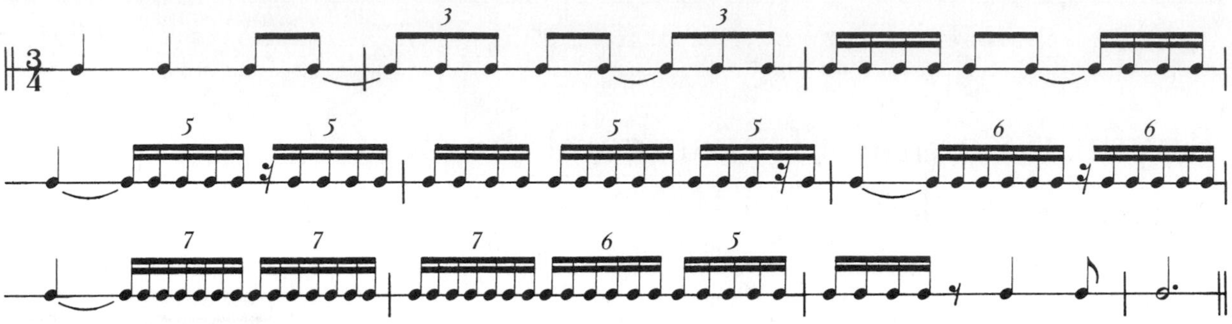

9.

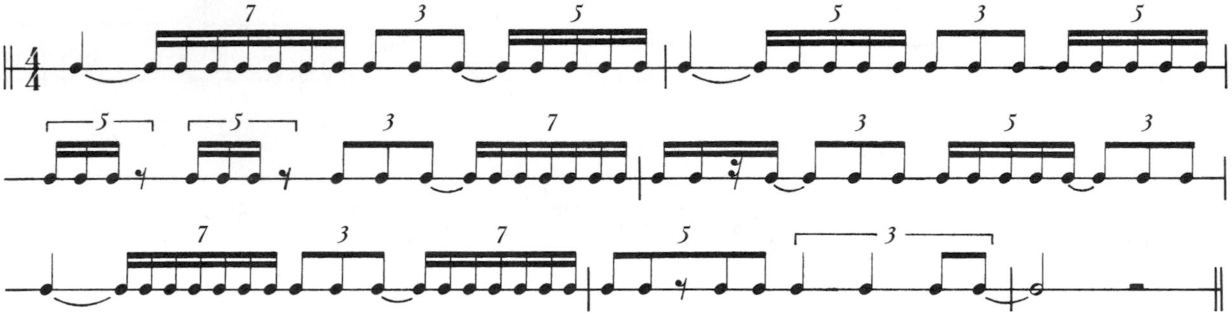

10.

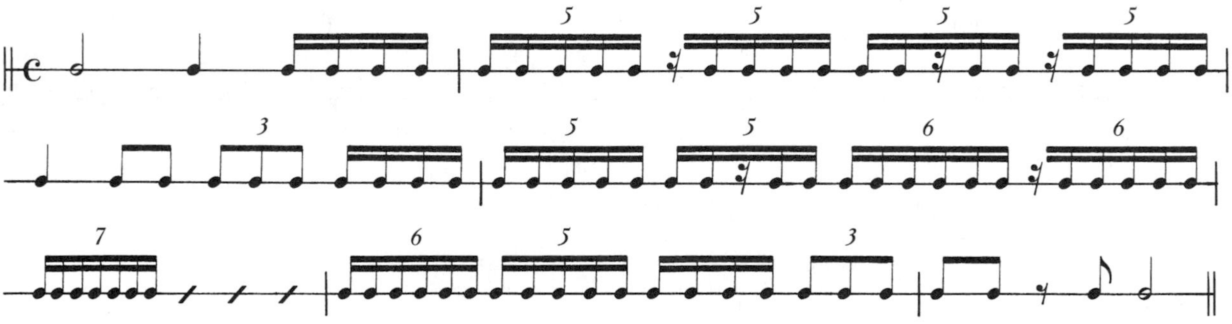

11.

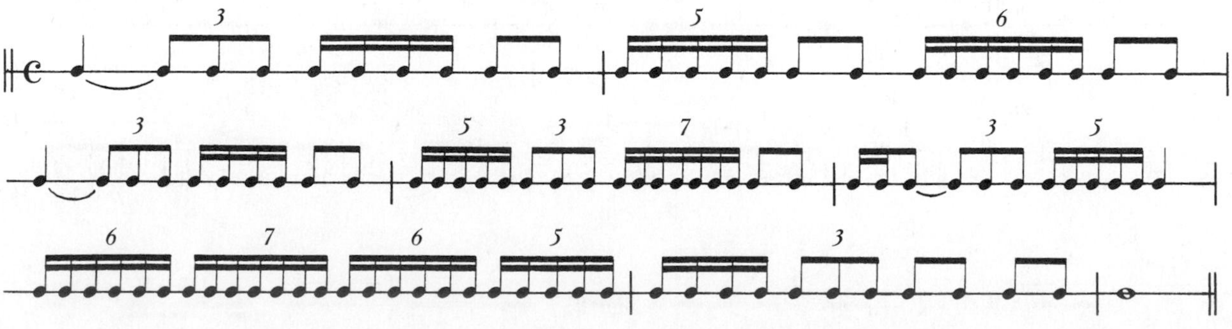

Pitch: Quartal Harmony

Preliminary Exercises

5.

6.

7.

8.

9.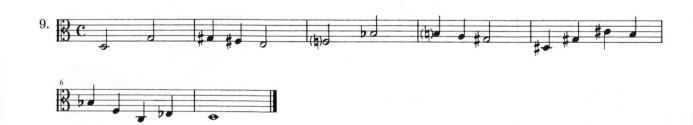

Melodies

Appassionato e molto espressivo

Part Music

Grazioso

2.

23

Rhythm: Polyrhythms and Polymeters

Preliminary Exercises

Pitch: Polyharmony and Polytonality

Part Music

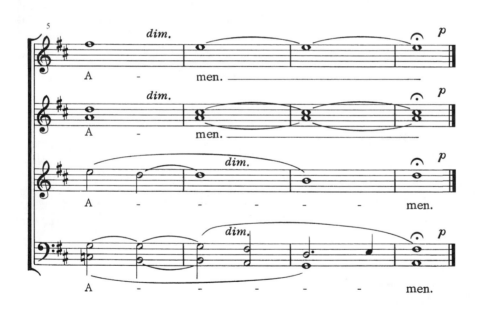

Firmly, not too fast

Let Your Light Shine

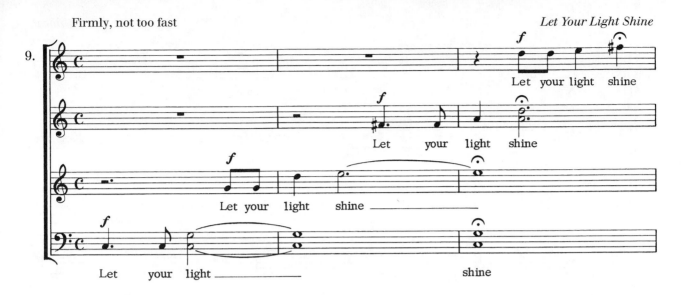

Slow, hushed *Amen!*

10.

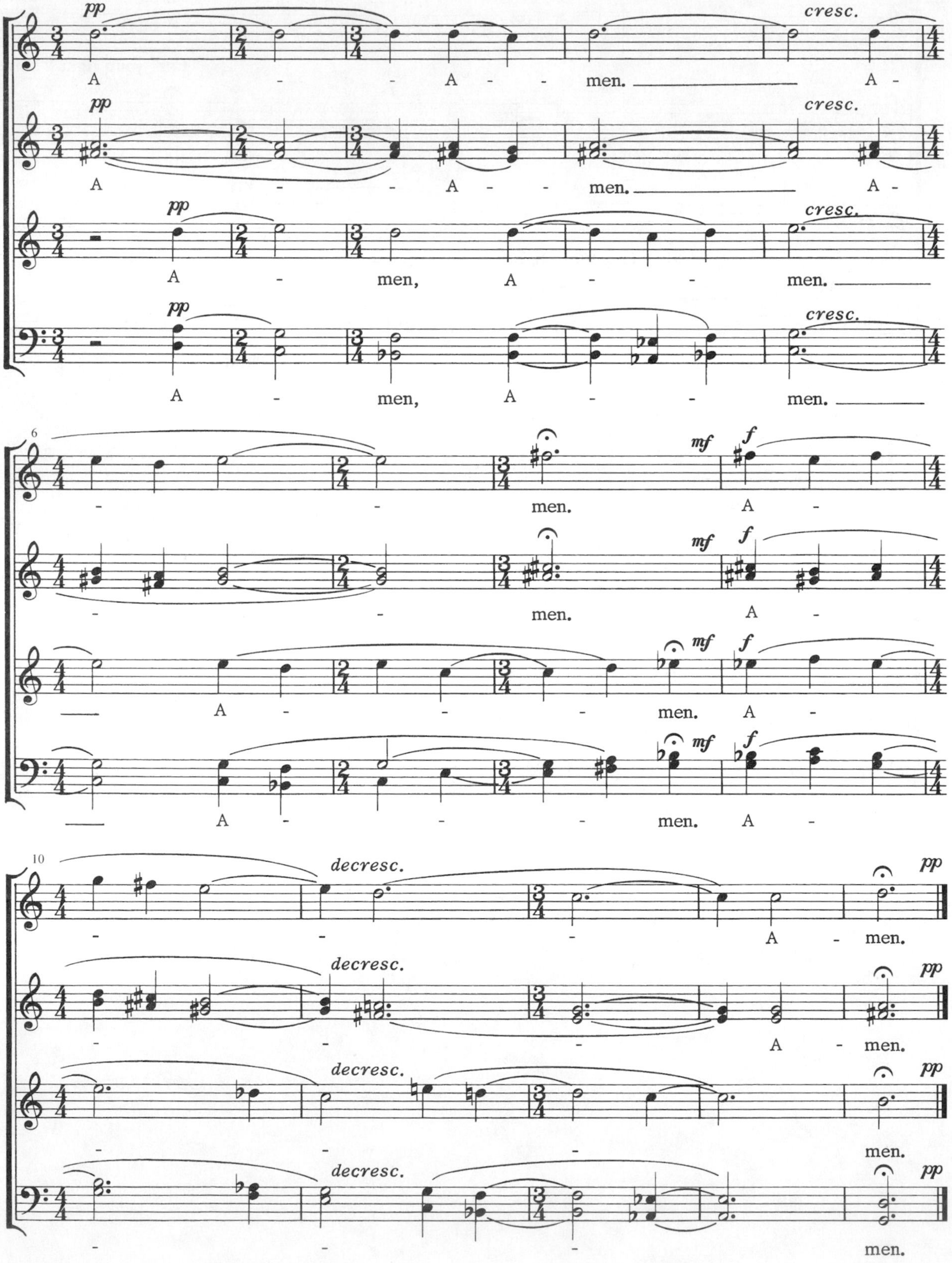

Brillante

11.

24

Pitch: Interval Music

Preliminary Exercises

Analyzing these exercises for linear tendencies and melodic and interval patterning will be helpful. Try to retain recurring pitches as reference points. These will often be first and last pitches or the principal pitch of any given segment.

8.

9.

10.

11.

12.

13.

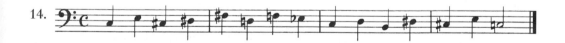

14.

15.

Melodies

Walzer

7.

Energico

8.

Medium swing

9.

Duets

Night music

1.

25

Serial Music

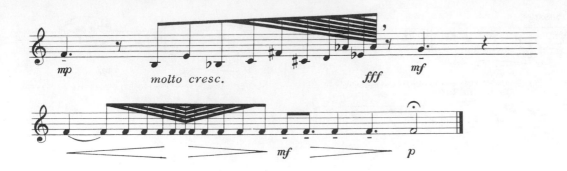

26

Music from the Literature

The following choral pieces are suggested for sight reading and ensemble performance in class. They represent a broad survey of techniques and materials found in twentieth-century music.

Reincarnations, Samuel Barber

Four Slavonic Folk Songs, Béla Bartók

Three Psalms of Celebration, Thomas Benjamin

Hymn to St. Cecilia, Benjamin Britten

Rejoice in the Lamb, Benjamin Britten

Trois Chansons, Claude Debussy

Singet den Herrn, Hugo Distler

Six Chansons, Paul Hindemith

A Child's Journey, Michael Horvit

Psalm 67, Charles Ives

Lux Aeterna, Györgi Ligeti

O sacrum convivium!, Olivier Messiaen

Madrigals for a New Age, Robert Nelson

Te Deum, Krzysztof Penderecki

Mass, Vincent Persichetti

Easter Cantata, Daniel Pinkham

De Profundis, Arnold Schoenberg

Friede auf Erden, Arnold Schoenberg

Carols of Death, William Schuman

Anthem, The Dove Descending, Igor Stravinsky

Ave Maria, Igor Stravinsky

Silence and Music, Ralph Vaughn Williams

Glossary

Accelerando (Accel.) (It.) becoming faster

Adagietto (It.) see *Tempo*

Adagio (It.) see *Tempo*

Agile (Fr.) agile, nimble

À la, Alla in the style or manner of

Allegretto (It.) see *Tempo*

Allegro (It.) see *Tempo*

Amabile (It.) amiable, graceful

Amore (It.) love
   Con amore with tenderness

Amoroso (It.) tender and affectionate

Andante (It.) see *Tempo*

Andantino (It.) see *Tempo*

Anima (It.), *Con anima* with life and animation, alt. soulful

Animato (It.), *Animé* (Fr.) animated, with life or spirit

Appassionato (It.) passionately, with intense emotion

Assai (It.) very, extremely, much

Assez (Fr.) enough, sufficiently

Ausdrucksvoll (Ger.) expressively

Avec (Fr.) with

Ballabile (It.) in the style of a dance

Barbaro (It.) barbarous, primitive

Barcarolle (Fr.) boat song

Ben (It.) much

Bewegt (Ger.) with movement

Bien (Fr.) well, good

Breit (Ger.) broad

Brillante (It.) bright, brilliant

Brio (It.) vigor, animation, spirit

Buffo (It.) in a comic style

Calando (It.) gradually softer and slower

Calmo (It.) calm, tranquil

Calore (It.) warmth, animation

Cantabile (It.) in a singing or lyrical style

Comodo (It.) easy, agreeable, comfortable

Con (It.) with

Da capo (D.C.) (It.) repeat from the beginning
   D.C. al Fine repeat from the beginning and play to the ending (*Fine*)

Dal Segno (D.S.) (It.) repeat from the sign (%)

Deciso (It.) boldly, decisively

Deliberatamente (It.) deliberately

Delicato (It.) delicate

Desto (It.) brisk, sprightly

Détaché (Fr.) detached, non legato

Dolce (It.) sweetly, softly

Dolore (It.) grief, sorrow

Doloroso (It.) sorrowfully, sadly

E, et and

Ecclesiastico (It.) of the church
   Nel modo ecclesiastico in the manner of church music

Edel (Ger.) noble

Einfach (Ger.) simple

En allant (Fr.) with movement

Energico (It.) energetic

Erhaben (Ger.) sublime, in a lofty and exalted style

Ernste (Ger.) serious, earnest, gravely

Eroico (It.) heroic

Espressione (It.) expression, feeling

Espressivo (It.) expressive
Etwas (Ger.) somewhat

Feierlich (Ger.) solemn, festive
Fine (It.) the end
Flessibile (It.) flexible, pliant
Fliessend (Ger.) flowing
Fort (Fr.) strong
Forza (It.) force, strength, power
Fröhlich (Ger.) joyous, happy
Fuoco (It.) fire
   Con fuoco with energy or passion
Furioso (It.) furious

Gai (Fr.) gay, merry
Geist (Ger.) spirit
   Mit Geist with soul or sentiment
Gemütlich (Ger.) agreeable, genial
Gesangvoll (Ger.) lyrical
Geschleift (Ger.) legato, connected
Geschwind (Ger.) quick, rapid
Giochévole (It.) merry, sportive
Giocoso, Giojoso (It.) humorous, jocose
Giusto (It.) steady, exact, alt. moderate
Gondellied (Ger.) boat song
Gracieux, Gracieusement (Fr.), *Grazioso* (It.) graceful
Grave (It.) see *Tempo*
Gross (Ger.) great amount, large

Heftig (Ger.) vehement, boisterous
Hurtig (Ger.) quick, swiftly

Incalzando (It.) getting faster and louder
Innig (Ger.) sincerely, with depth of feeling
Innocente (It.) innocently

Jolie (Fr.) pleasant, pretty

Keck (Ger.) pert, fearless, bold
Klar (Ger.) clear, bright
Klingend (Ger.) sonorous, ringing
Kraft (Ger.) strength, power
Kräftig (Ger.) powerfully, vigorously
Kurz (Ger.) short, detached, staccato

Ländler (Ger.) country dance, in a rustic and popular style
Langsam (Ger.) slow
Larghetto (It.) see *Tempo*
Largo (It.) see *Tempo*
Lebhaft (Ger.) lively
Legato (It.) connected, smoothly
Leggiero (It.) light, delicate
Leicht (Ger.) lightly
Lentamente (It.), *Lentement* (Fr.) slowly
Lento (It.), *Lent* (Fr.) see *Tempo*
Lieblich (Ger.) lovely, delightful
Liscio (It.) simple, smooth
Lugubre (Fr., It.) sad, mournful
Lustig (Ger.) merrily, cheerfully

Maestoso (It.) majestic, stately
Marcato (It.) marked, accented

Marziale (It.) martial, in the style of a march
Mässig (Ger.) moderate (see *Tempo*)
Melancholique (Fr.) melancholy
Meno (It.) less
Mesto (It.) sad, mournful
Misura (It.) measure
   Senza misura without measure, freely
Mit (Ger.) with
Moderato (It.), *Modéré* (Fr.) see *Tempo*
Molto (It.) much, a great amount
Morendo (It.) dying away
Mosso, Moto (It.), *Mouvement* (Fr.) motion, movement
   Avec mouvement (Fr.) with motion
   Con moto (It.) with motion, rather quick
Munter (Ger.) lively, merry

Non (It.) not
Nostalgico (It.) nostalgic

Ostinato (It.) obstinate, continuing

Passionato (It.) passionate
Passione (It.) passion, feeling
Perdendosi (It.) dying away
Pesante (It.) heavy, ponderous
Piacevole (It.) pleasing, agreeable
Più (It.) more
Placido (It.) placid, calm
Poco (It.) a little
   Poco a poco gradually
Polacca (It.) a Polish dance
Pomposo (It.) pompous, grand
Prestissimo (It.) see *Tempo*
Presto (It.) see *Tempo*

Rallentando (Rall.) (It.) becoming gradually slower
Rasch (Ger.) very fast, swift, spirited
Religioso (It.) religiously, solemn
Retenu (Fr.) held back
Risoluto (It.) resolved, resolute, bold
Ritard (Rit.) (It.) becoming gradually slower
Ritmico (It.) rhythmically
Rubato (It.) freely with respect to tempo
Ruhig (Ger.) quiet, calm
Rustico (It.) rural, rustic, coarse

Scherzando (It.) playful, lively
Schleppend (Ger.) dragging
Schmerzvollisch (Ger.) painfully, dolorous
Schnell (Ger.) fast
   Nicht zu schnell (Ger.) not too fast
   So schnell wie möglich as fast as possible
Schwerigkeit (Ger.) heaviness, seriousness, severity, difficulty
Schwungvoll (Ger.) animated, spirited
Sehnsucht (Ger.) desire, ardor, longing, fervor
Sehr (Ger.) very
Semplice (It.) simple
Sempre (It.) always, continuously
Sentimentale (It.) sentimentally
Sentimento (It.) sentimental

Sentito (It.) expressive
Senza (It.) without
Serioso (It.) serious
Siciliano (It.) graceful movement of a pastoral character
Simile (It.) similarly, continue in the same manner
Slancio (It.) vehemence
   Con slancio (It.) impetuously
Solenne (It.) solemn
Sordamente (It.) muted, softly
Sospirando (It.) sighing, doleful
Sostenuto (It.) sustained, legato
Sotto voce (It.) softly, in a subdued manner
Spasshaft (Ger.) jokingly, playfully
Spirito (It.) spirit, energy
Spiritoso (It.) with spirit, energetic
Spirituoso (It.) with religious feeling
Squillante (It.) ringing
Stark (Ger.) strong, vigorous, loud
   So stark wie möglich as strong as possible

Tempo (It.) time, relative speed or rate of the pulse or beat
   A tempo (It.) once again in time

   Chart of Relative Tempos
   M.M.

40	Grave
	Largo
	Larghetto
	Lento
60	Adagio
	Adagietto
72	Andante
	Andantino
90	Moderato
	Allegretto
120	Allegro
140	Presto
208	Prestissimo

Tenuto (It.) sustained, held out
Trascinando (It.) dragging
Trés (Fr.) very
Troppo (It.) much
   Non troppo not too much

Valse (Fr.) waltz
Vienne (Fr.) Vienna
   À la vienne in the style of a Viennese waltz
Vif (Fr.) lively
Vite (Fr.) fast, quickly
Vivace (It.) lively
Volkston, Im Volkston (Ger.) in the manner of a folksong

Walzer (Ger.) waltz
Wuth (Ger.) madness, rage

Zart (Ger.) gently, sweetly, tender, soft
Zeitmass (Ger.) tempo
   Im Zeitmass in tempo
Zierlich (Ger.) neat, graceful
Zurückhaltend (Ger.) ritard